# NORTH MARKET
# COOKBOOK

## RECIPES & STORIES FROM COLUMBUS OHIO's Historic Public Market

BY **MICHAEL**TURBACK
FOREWORD BY **ROBIN DAVIS**

FARM FRESH BOOKS
www.farmfreshbooks.com

For sales visit: www.farmfreshbooks.com

ISBN: 978-0-9787368-1-1

FOREWORD BY ROBIN DAVIS
PHOTOGRAPHS BY KEN HEIGEL AND TOM HOGAN
BOOK DESIGN BY ART & ANTHROPOLOGY, INC.
CONSULTING CHEF  LARRY CHISZAR
PRINTED IN THE UNITED STATES OF AMERICA

**FIRST PRINTING**

## THIS BOOK IS DEDICATED TO DAVID WIBLE

whose leadership guided the North Market on a journey of growth from 2000 — 2013.

We gratefully acknowledge the support of:

**Rick Harrison Wolfe**
*Executive Director*

**Peggy Outcalt**
*Director of Operations*

**Mary Martineau**
*Director of Marketing*

**Amy Summers**
*Office Manager*

We applaud their passion for and dedication to the North Market.

They make it all happen.

# FOREWORD

When I first moved to Columbus more than ten years ago, I met with the then-food editor at the *Dispatch* to get her inside scoop on the food scene.

"You have to go to the North Market," was the first thing she said.

I have been a regular at the Market ever since.

My career in food writing has led me to many public markets: the Farmers Market in Los Angeles, Ferry Plaza in San Francisco and West Side Market in Cleveland. But it's with the North Market that I feel a special connection.

I'm drawn in by the vendors – the farmers and merchants – selling what they grow and make. They're artisans, every one, producing some of the best foods customers can get in Ohio.

Jeni Britton Bauer started Jeni's Splendid Ice Creams at the North Market and has gone on to be wildly successful nationwide, including with a best-selling cookbook that she's often referred to as her "love letter to Ohio."

The North Market is a kind of love letter, too. Innovative people sell what they believe in, what they love, whether its hand-twisted pretzels, hot sauces of every variety or meats from animals they've raised themselves.

The North Market had a vibrant farmers market before they became trendy, and still packs in farmers – and customers – every Saturday morning for some of the best fruits and vegetables to be found anywhere.

But the magic of the North Market is more than what's available for purchase. It's about the history. For more than 100 years, the Market has been part of the Columbus community.

It's also about the customers. Whenever I visit, I see local chefs looking for ingredients to serve at their restaurants.

And I see friends, like-minded people as devoted to the flavors and foods of Ohio as I am. I started going to the North Market on another food lover's suggestion. But now I'm the one making the recommendation.

"You're coming to Columbus? You have to go to the North Market."

— **Robin Davis**
*author and former food editor at the* Columbus Dispatch

*"One of the very nicest things about life is the way we must regularly stop whatever it is we are doing and devote our attention to eating."*

— Luciano Pavarotti

# PRELUDE

In Ohio's capital, as in many other cities throughout 19th century America, public markets were the primary channels of perishable food distribution.

The Columbus Central Market was built in 1850 at Fourth Street, on the city block between Town and Rich Streets, followed by West Market, on South Gift Street, and East Market, at the intersection of Mt. Vernon and Miami Avenues. The original North End Market (as it was called then), at Spruce and High Streets on the city's north side, was erected in 1876. In addition to merchants who had their stalls in the handsome market houses, other venders set up stands along surrounding streets. By 1917, public markets attracted 125,000 weekly shoppers, three-fourths of the city's population.

These locations became vibrant centers for exchange among the city's residents and tradespeople as well as the beginning of consumption as a social activity. Foodstuffs were carried into the city and offered for sale or barter. Shoppers arrived on foot or by buggy. It was a time when most Ohioans earned their living off of the land and when local farmers grew local food for local folks. Yet the march of "progress" would bring about a change in agriculture and a change in distribution networks.

After World War II, food production and trade were corporatized and expanded to a national scale, and supermarkets began eclipsing the old municipal market houses. New neighborhood business districts emerged in the suburbs while the automobile altered lifestyles – and the shape of Columbus itself. While the city's other venues faded into memory, the North Market survived a disastrous fire in 1947 and emerged from the ashes into a pre-fabricated Quonset hut purchased by merchants who soldiered on.

In 1982, the North Market District was nominated to the National Register of Historic Places by the Columbus Landmarks Foundation. Ten years later, with the support of preservationists and other advocates, the North Market Development Authority negotiated a lease with the city for the former Advanced-Rumely

Thresher farm machinery warehouse just behind the Market's original High Street location. A capital campaign was undertaken to finance building renovations, and the re-opening of a restored and revitalized North Market in November of 1995 proved to be a catalyst for downtown regeneration.

It's no longer a relic of the past. Revival of commerce at the site now represents everything that's best about a marketplace where community is served. Columbus has embraced today's North Market as an indelible part of its identity, a civic amenity, and one of the most colorful threads in its cultural tapestry. As the city's only surviving public market, it is an incubator of food entrepreneurship and showcase for locally grown or produced goods. Its importance lies as much in its aspiration as in its considerable achievement.

Inside the public hall, three dozen independent merchants include butchers, bakers and ice cream makers, greengrocers, restaurateurs and purveyors of everything from exotic spices to practical cookware. And throughout the growing season, the outdoors comes alive in a whirlwind of open-air commerce, an extraordinary exhibition of local bounty.

This is daily theater, with ever-fresh performances daily – a primal Columbus experience. People gather, gossip over coffee, indulge in people-watching and blissful eating. Parents push kids in strollers. Buckeye fans stock up for tailgate parties. Regulars come armed with canvas bags and wicker baskets to haul away weekly buys. Local chefs prowl for carefully-sourced ingredients. Out-of-towners stare with curiosity and admiration.

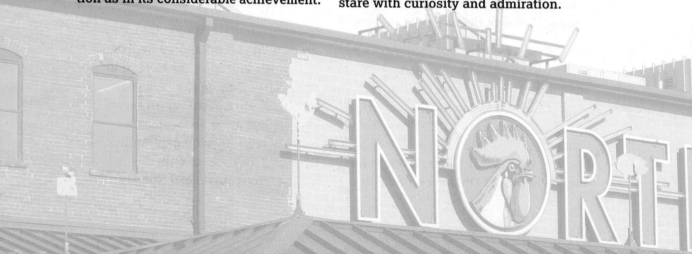

In its own way, the North Market defines the character of Columbus. It has become one of the most influential enterprises of its kind in the country, a well-supported community gathering place, routinely attracting perhaps the most socially, economically, racially, and ethnically diverse crowds found anywhere in the region. Few shopping experiences compare to wandering the Market – both in terms of sensory impressions or of human interactions. And as it has throughout its long life, the Market continues to provide reliable income for the independent vendors, as well as fresh, affordable food for locals and tourists alike.

This anthology is meant to celebrate the North Market's resounding impact on the way we eat, so let's give credit where it's due – to the family of merchants who inspire the jumble of sights, sounds, and smells that are part of an urban food shopping destination and a beacon of deliciousness like no other. You will meet many of them as soon as you begin leafing through this book. You are about to read their behind-the-scenes stories.

When it comes right down to it, of course, this is also a collection of delectable and inventive recipes. Many provide a grassroots connection to farms and fields surrounding the city. Some will feel familiar to you by the nature of their simple techniques; others will require curiosity and a sense of adventure. It's a grouping as diversified and provocative as the Market itself.

If after reading the stories and sampling the recipes, you feel that you have not only eaten well, but better understand the vitality and importance of a place like the North Market, then I'll have succeeded.

**–MICHAEL TURBACK**
LOCAVORE and RACONTEUR

A Touch Of Earth
Best Of The Wurst
Better Earth
Bluescreek Farm Meats
Brēzel
Bubbles The Tea & Juice Company
CaJohns Flavor & Fire
Curds & Whey
Expressly Market Bakery And Bistro
Firdous Express
Flavors Of India
Heil's Family Deli
Holy Smoke Bbq
Hubert's Polish Kitchen
Jeni's Splendid Ice Creams
Lan Viet Market
Market Blooms
Nida's Sushi
North Market Cookware
North Market Poultry And Game
North Market Spices
Omega Artisan Baking
Pam's Market Popcorn
Pastaria
Pure Imagination Chocolatier
Sarefino's Pizzeria And Italian Deli
Taste Of Belgium
The Barrel & Bottle
The Fish Guys
The Greener Grocer
The Source By Wasserstrom

# A TOUCH
## of earth

**To some, coffee is coffee,** but to others it's an experience unto itself. Coffee is a social mainstay at the North Market – make your way to a gathering place at the center of the hall where friends catch up with one another while baristas put finishing touches on artful drinks.

Ann Leonard practically grew up at the Market. "My grandparents were the poultry purveyors, and I worked for them," she explains. "But I had my eye on the shop across from our stand called A Touch of Earth. When I purchased the business it was all about things that came from the earth – grains, herbs, spices, beans, and yes, coffee beans." As focus narrowed over the years, A Touch of Earth emerged as the go-to destination for the city's best coffee.

Truth be told, the secret of a damn good cup of coffee is freshness, both in the preparation and in the roasting of the carefully chosen beans – roasting unlocks and frames a coffee's flavor potential. "We're lucky to have some incredibly talented, small-batch roasters here in Columbus," says Ann, "and we only use beans that have been roasted within seven days, so the flavors are still lively." "You can tell a lot about a city by its coffee culture," she explains, "and by that standard, boy, people get serious about coffee here." She's supported by Noah, Adele, Jamaal, and Lucy, a team of baristas whose ritual with the meticulous extraction technique called "pour over" keeps local coffee devotees abuzz. Coffee is treated like an art, or at least a high form of craft. Beans are ground to order for each cup. Milk from Snowville Creamery is steamed to order from an arsenal of small steam pitchers. And pastries from Pâtisserie Lallier provide companionship to superb espressos.

Pour yourself into the experience by heading over to A Touch of Earth. Then sit and chat with friends, read today's *Dispatch*, or work on your laptop. To drink coffee here is to join the rhythm of the Market. If you're planning a visit, give your home coffee-maker a rest.

# Caffè con Cioccolato

*makes 4 servings*

In the Italian city of Turin, the blending of chocolate and coffee is a ritual, an enthusiasm, and in the case of bicerin (pronounced bee-chair-EEN), an obsession. The pairing of ingredients, despite its apparent simplicity, is an alliance of perfect proportions. With one part espresso, one part chocolate, and one part cream, it is a feat of culinary engineering. To compose the showpiece, each ingredient is poured carefully into a tempered glass, creating not only visually enchanting layers of liquids, but a sequence of vigorous taste sensations in culinary harmony.

## THE HOT CHOCOLATE

6 **ounces whole milk**
3 **ounces bittersweet chocolate,**
   **finely chopped**
   **dash of salt**

**1.** Heat milk slowly over low heat, stirring frequently, until steaming, being careful not to scorch it.

**2.** Add the chopped chocolate and salt to the steaming milk. Stir slowly over low heat, not allowing mixture to boil. Remove from heat.

## THE DRINK

8 **ounces espresso**
   **hot chocolate (from left)**
   **lightly-sweetened whipped cream**

Using each of 4 tempered short-stem glasses, pour in 2 ounces of hot, freshly pulled espresso; layer 2 ounces of the warm chocolate on top of each espresso by pouring down the bottom of a tablespoon held against the side of the glass to create a separate layer; again using a tablespoon, pour an equal layer of cream over the top of each drink.

**NOTE** *The cream should be hand-whipped to a consistency just thick enough to float on top of the drink.*

While Europeans use coffee like a final punctuation mark to a meal, Americans drink coffee along with dessert – even the coffee break often includes a cookie or pastry.

As natural bedfellows, chocolate and coffee both run the gamut from light to dark, from bitter to sweet, and, when blended together in a creative dessert, add grown-up sophistication to the table. Michelle Kozak of Pâtisserie Lallier, who provides many of the coffee-friendly pastries to the North Market's coffee bar, shares her recipe for these Proustian, shell-shaped treats, crafted with a delightful marriage of chocolate and coffee.

# Chocolate-Espresso MADELEINES

*makes 12 servings*

## THE GLAZE

| | |
|---|---|
| 1 | tablespoon freshly brewed espresso |
| 1 3/4 | cups powdered sugar |
| 3 | tablespoons warm water |

Combine the espresso, powdered sugar, and water in a bowl and whisk to blend.

## THE MADELEINES

| | |
|---|---|
| 6 | tablespoons butter + 1 tablespoon for preparing the pan |
| 1/4 | cup freshly brewed espresso |
| 1/4 | cup semi-sweet chocolate |
| 3/4 | cup flour |
| 1/3 | cup sugar |
| 2 | eggs |
| 1 | teaspoon baking powder |
| 1/2 | cup roughly-chopped dark chocolate espresso glaze (from left) |

1. In a small pan on the stove, combine the butter, espresso, and semi-sweet chocolate. Put the pan on a low heat/simmer setting to allow the ingredients to slowly melt.

2. In a bowl, combine the flour, sugar, eggs and baking powder and mix lightly until just combined. When the butter mixture has melted completely, add it to the flour mixture and stir lightly. Add the chopped chocolate, and mix a few times to integrate it. Be careful not to over mix the batter. Place the bowl in the refrigerator for 2 hours or up to 2 days, covering it with foil or plastic wrap.

3. When ready to bake, set the oven to 375° F., and butter/flour a madeleine pan. Remove batter from the refrigerator, and scoop it into a pastry bag or a large plastic baggie. Cut the tip off, and pipe the batter into the Madeleine molds. Place the pan in the oven and bake for about 13 minutes or until the tops of the cakes spring back when lightly touched.

4. Remove the pan from the oven, let sit for 1 minute in the pan, and then turn out onto a cooling rack. As soon as they are cool enough to handle, dip each cake in the glaze, turning over to make sure both sides are coated, and wipe excess off sides. After dipping, rest each one back on the cooling rack, scalloped side up, until the cakes are cool and the glaze has firmed up. They are best eaten the day they're made.

**Given that patrons are literally surrounded by bottles,** in every imaginable style and price range, the Barrel and Bottle is uniquely suited to beer and wine lovers of every stripe.

"For some people, wine can be intimidating, but it doesn't have to be," says Jen Burton, whose passion for wine was ignited as a server at the Spagio Wine Lounge. And her business partner, Collin Castore, has become something of a craft beer savant as partner in Bodega, a Short North café that takes its brews seriously. You might call their Market venture a marriage of two passions.

With a team that's knowledgeable and enthusiastic, the folks at Barrel and Bottle make great effort to appeal to the casual wine drinker. "More than a third of our inventory falls into that sweet-spot range between $10 and $15," says Jen. And when marketgoers seek a suitable bottle to accompany takeout, she stands ready for any wine-pairing challenge. "Matching many of the dishes from our vendors is an interesting intellectual process," she admits. "With spice-driven, ethnic dishes, the key is often a bit of residual sugar to round out the sharp edges – an Ohio-grown, semi-dry Riesling from Ferrante Winery might be just the thing."

And, on the other hand, a local craft beer might provide even more versatility. "An extra layer of carbonation cleanses the palate," explains Collin, "and you can run the gamut from bitter to sweet, pale to dark, light to full-bodied." He pitches the citrusy, fragrant character of Columbus Brewing Company's IPA to compliment a wide range of foods.

Jen and Collin sell the beers and wines they love, and in the process they have built a cadre of loyalists who repeatedly patronize their shop. They take a fun and friendly approach, one that fits the convivial nature of the Market.

the barrel
& BOT

Even though he has never set foot on Belgian soil, Chef Marcus Andrew Meacham of Bodega doesn't let that detail infringe on his right to revamp one of the country's national dishes. In his *moules à la crème*, the wine imparts a pleasant acidity, but his version also has flavorful add-ins – bacon, onion, garlic, and blue cheese – clinging to the mussels, and a pinch of pepper flakes for zest.

According to Collin, the dish goes famously with Rock Mill Saison, an organic farmhouse ale from Lancaster. "It's light and peppery so as not to overpower the mussels," he explains, "but with enough earth in the yeast character to balance out the richness of the broth."

# BEST-EVER
# Mussels & Frites

*makes 2 servings*

## THE FRITES

| | |
|---|---|
| 2 | medium russet potatoes (about 1 3/4 pounds), unpeeled |
| 2 | tablespoons canola oil |
| 2 | garlic cloves, minced |
| 1/2 | teaspoon salt |
| 1 | tablespoon finely-chopped parsley |

**1.** Preheat the oven to 450° F. Heat the garlic and oil in a small saucepan over medium heat for 2 minutes. Strain the garlic from the oil with a small mesh strainer. Set both garlic and oil aside.

**2.** Cut the potatoes into ¼" sticks. In a large bowl, toss the oil, potatoes and salt. Spread the potatoes onto an oiled baking sheet in a single layer. Bake until golden and crisp, about 35 minutes.

**3.** Transfer potatoes to a bowl and toss with parsley, reserved garlic, and additional salt, to taste.

## THE DISH

| | |
|---|---|
| 12 | mussels |
| 1/4 | cup bacon lardons, cooked |
| 2 | tablespoons red onion, diced |
| 2 | tablespoons garlic, minced |
| 1/2 | teaspoon crushed red pepper flakes |
| 1/4 | cup dry white wine |
| 1/4 | cup heavy cream |
| 1/2 | cup bleu cheese crumbles+ more for garnish |
| 2 | tablespoons butter |
| 1/4 | cup fresh parsley, chopped |

**1.** Heat a sauté pan over medium high heat. Add the mussels, bacon and red onion and cook for 2 minutes. Add the garlic and red pepper flakes and stir. Add the wine, cream and bleu cheese and stir. Cover the pan and reduce heat to medium. Allow the mussels to cook in the sauce covered for 4 to 5 minutes until the mussels open and their flesh is cooked through.

**2.** Stir in the butter, to finish the sauce. Arrange the mussels in a ring around the outside of a bowl and stuff the fries in the center between them. Pour the sauce over the mussels and the fries. Garnish with parsley and more blue cheese crumbles and a pinch of crushed red pepper.

NOTE *Discard any mussels that do not open.*

# Champagne-Braised
# JICAMA SALAD

*makes 4 servings*

Jicama tastes like a crunchy cross between mild radishes and water chestnuts. In Chef Meacham's salad, braising intermingles those flavors with the bright, subtle flavors of the cooking liquid. Pairing this dish with Columbus Brewing Company's seasonal Summerteeth, Collin explains, "The crisp unfiltered Kellerbier has slightly more hop than your average lager which allows it to stand up to this fresh and flavorful salad."

## BRAISED JICAMA

| | |
|---|---|
| 4 | pounds Jicama, peeled and cut into 1" cubes |
| 2 | cups dry white wine |
| 1/2 | cup champagne vinegar |
| 1 | tablespoon celery seeds |
| 1/2 | cup onions, diced |
| 2 | tablespoons garlic, minced |

Preheat oven to 400°. Heat oil in a shallow oven-safe pan until very hot. Add jicama cubes and sear on each side. Season the jicama with salt and pepper. Add remaining ingredients and bring to a boil. Slide the pan into the oven uncovered. Allow the jicama to braise for 45 minutes. Remove jicama cubes and chill. Pass the remaining braising liquid through a fine mesh strainer or coffee filter. Chill and reserve.

## PICKLED RED ONIONS

| | |
|---|---|
| 1 | red onion, very thinly sliced |
| 1 | cup red wine vinegar |
| 1 | tablespoon peppercorns |
| 2 | bay leaves |
| 3 | cloves garlic |

In a sauce pan, combine all ingredients except the red onions and bring to a boil. Allow mixture to simmer for 5 minutes. Place the onions in a bowl or plastic container. Pour the vinegar mixture through a fine mesh strainer onto the onions and stir. Cover the onions allow to cool to room temperature. Chill and reserve.

## THE DRESSING

Combine 1/3 cup of chilled braising liquid with 2/3 cup extra virgin olive oil.

## THE SALAD

| | |
|---|---|
| 16 | ounces mixed baby greens |
| | dressing (from above) |
| | salt |
| | black pepper, freshly-cracked |
| | braised jicama cubes (from left) |
| 1 | cucumber, thinly sliced |
| | pickled red onions (from left) |

1. In a large bowl, toss greens with a small amount of dressing, just to coat. (Use your hands to massage the delicate leaves with dressing). Season with salt and pepper to taste.

2. To serve, divide the greens among 4 chilled salad plates. Arrange jicama cubes, cucumber slices and pickled onions on top of the greens; pass extra dressing alongside.

# best
## OF THE WURST

**The American table is a melting pot** of many different cultures and cuisines. As immigrants brought traditions and food from their countries, they made an impact at the American table. The influence of German immigrants who settled in large numbers in Columbus has been kept alive at the North Market.

With the success of Nida's Sushi (see page 82), owners Nida and Chris Perry agreed to carry on the legacy of the "wurst man" at the North Market with the purchase of Best of the Wurst in 2002. "I had to make the long walk back and forth, back and forth all day between the two businesses," Nida says with a laugh, "until I moved them next to each other."

Of course, sausages are some of the first things that come to mind when one thinks of German cuisine, and she had a lot to learn about German sausage culture. "It was something completely different from my own background, both exciting and challenging," Nida admits, "and thank goodness for Market customers – they were my best teachers."

She was apparently a good student. Nida's irresistible all-beef hot dogs and sausages rotate on a rotisserie, then with each order, finished on an Italian panini machine. Nestled in a bun, they literally burst with juicy flavor. Besides standard condiments, choices of cheese, cole slaw, chili, or sauerkraut complete each hand-held meal.

The menu is embellished with a wide range of other sandwiches pressed on the panini grill, elevating ordinary sandwiches into layered specialties with crunchy crusts and creative deli fillings, served warm and oozing with cheese.

According to Columbus culinary folklore, this pretzel sandwich was once the specialty of The Place Upstairs in German Village. Pairing Best of the Wurst brats with Brēzel soft pretzels breathes new life into this nearly-forgotten recipe. In addition, cheese from Curds and Whey plus spicy mustard from CaJohn's add two more North Market-sourced components. Wunderbar!

# Brünhilde ON A BRĒZEL

*makes 1 sandwich*

## SANDWICH

| | |
|---|---|
| 1 | tablespoon butter, softened |
| 1 | tablespoon olive oil |
| 1 | large soft pretzel, sliced in half horizontally |
| 1 | tablespoon CaJohn's "Dog-On Good" or other spicy mustard |
| 4 | slices Monterey Jack cheese |
| 1 | bratwurst, grilled and sliced lengthwise |
| 1/4 | cup sauerkraut |
| | black pepper, fresh-cracked |

1. Heat butter and olive oil in a large frying pan over medium-low heat. Spread the inside of the pretzel halves with mustard and place in the pan, crust side down. Arrange the slices of cheese to cover both halves. Heat the pretzels until the cheese begins to melt.

NOTE *Do not "over-melt" the cheese in the pan, or it will "drip" through the pretzel openings.*

2. Remove cheese-covered pretzel halves from the pan. Place sliced bratwurst on one half and top with the sauerkraut. Add pepper to taste. Close the sandwich with the other half of the pretzel.

Attention Buckeye tailgaters! Serve your pre-game hot dogs with an unexpected topper, made with fresh ingredients from the Market.

The beauty of this Southern-inspired slaw is that you can make it different every time, adding other vegetables including red or green tomatoes, carrots, beans, asparagus, cauliflower, or peas. If this sounds messy, be assured that architecturally speaking, the worst that can happen is that a little bit falls into your lap.

# CHOW-CHOW for Hot Dogs

*makes 6–8 servings*

## CONDIMENT

| | |
|---|---|
| 1 1/2 | cups cider vinegar |
| 1 | cup sugar |
| 2 | teaspoons celery seeds |
| 2 | teaspoons mustard seeds |
| 2 | teaspoons dry mustard |
| 1 | teaspoon turmeric |
| 1 | tablespoon salt |
| 1 | small head green cabbage, shredded |
| 1 | large sweet onion, finely chopped |
| 1 | red bell pepper, chopped |
| 2 | tablespoons olive oil |

**1.** In a medium-size saucepot, bring the cider vinegar, sugar, celery seeds, mustard seeds, dry mustard, turmeric, and salt to a boil.

**2.** Add the cabbage, onion, and bell pepper to the boiling mixture and simmer for about 10 minutes. Remove from heat. Pour the mixture into a large bowl, toss with the olive oil and let cool in the fridge.

**NOTE** *The Chow-Chow can be stored in the fridge for up to 2 weeks in a sealed container.*

**Remember the old general store?** It carried a broad selection of merchandise, usually in a small space, and it was where folks from the town and surrounding rural areas would come to purchase all their general goods. Well, here at the North Market, the traditional concept of the general store still exists, only now it serves a more enlightened lifestyle – filled with environmentally-friendly, socially-responsible, and delightfully-eccentric merchandise.

# BETTER earth

Her eco-friendly passions started with an interest in making a difference to the planet and joining Earth Day's 20th Birthday. The year was 1990 and Dareen Wearstler opened the first "ecology store" in Columbus, selling products that met one or more of these criteria: natural/organic materials, recycled and recyclable, biodegradable, fair trade, sustainable, reuseable, vegan, energy efficient, and water conserving.

What is remarkable about Better Earth is how true it is to Dareen's spirit. She explains that she was inspired by her personal passion for an eco-friendly and sustainable lifestyle. "I was looking for a way to marry that passion with a business."

"Folks at the North Market are extraordinarily willing to listen and consider my products," says Dareen, who has expanded her offerings to include personal care, aromatherapy, cleaning products, handmade soaps and artisan-made gift items. In addition, she's on a mission to support products that travel less than 100 miles to get to the store. Locally-made products are prominently displayed throughout the store.

Better Earth is a one-stop shop for almost every basic green need you can have. "I use the antique store theory," she explains. "The store is like a treasure chest with a lot of little gems – you just have to look around."

Levi and Wilma Yoder started a seasonal cider-pressing operation in the Knox County village of Gambier in 1975. In an effort to create a year-round business, the Amish family began producing apple butter, made from local orchard-grown apples, slow-cooked in kettles to coax out natural flavors. Explore the shelves at Better Earth for a jar of Yoder's Homemade Apple Butter, the not-so-secret ingredient in these home kitchen "hand forged" doughnuts, exceptionally good for dunking. (It is said that Ohio-born Clark Gable introduced the ritual of dipping and dunking doughnuts into coffee in the 1934 movie *It Happened One Night*).

# Amish Apple Butter
# DOUGHNUTS

*makes 12 doughnuts*

## DOUGHNUT

| | |
|---|---|
| 1/2 | cup sugar |
| 1 | egg |
| 2 | tablespoons butter, softened |
| 3/4 | cup Yoder's Homemade Apple Butter |
| 1/4 | cup maple syrup |
| 1/4 | cup buttermilk |
| 2 | cups all-purpose flour |
| 1 | teaspoon baking powder |
| 1/4 | teaspoon baking soda |
| 1/2 | teaspoon salt |
| | oil for deep-fat frying |

1. In a large bowl, beat together the sugar, eggs and butter with ¾ cup of apple butter, maple syrup and buttermilk. Sift the flour, baking powder, baking soda, and salt into the bowl of a stand mixer fitted with the dough hook attachment. On low speed, add the wet ingredients to the flour mixture. Continue mixing until the dough becomes smooth. Cover and refrigerate for at least 2 hours.

2. After the dough has rested, roll it out evenly to ¾" thickness. Cut out doughnuts using a floured doughnut cutter.

3. In an electric skillet or deep fryer, heat oil to 375° F. Fry doughnuts, a few at a time, until golden brown on both sides. Remove from the oil and drain on a paper-towel-lined plate

4. Serve warm or at room temperature.

**Local folks say** "the grass is greener" in Marysville, and that's where, smack dab on nearly eighty lush acres of rolling green pastureland, Cheryl and David Smith raise artisan livestock.

As lifelong farmers, the Smiths are true believers. Cheryl grew up on her family's Bluescreek Farm, and explains that "we're doing things the way our grandparents did them – we never changed." Besides allowing the animals to roam the abundant meadows, feed on succulent clusters of native grasses and drink from the pristine creek that flows through the property, diets are supplemented with farm-grown hay and a balanced ration of corn, oats, beanmeal, and minerals. "We never use growth stimulants, antibiotics, additives, steroids, or anything," she insists. "It's the old fashioned way."

At first, the Bluescreek herd of cattle was exclusively Belgian Blue, a distinct breed, often called the ultimate beef machine for its high proportion of valuable cuts. Over the years, cross-breeding with Piedmontese, Limousine, and Angus breeds has combined to improve early maturity, hardiness, and foraging ability. And more recently, the Smiths have expanded the farm family to include lambs, hogs, and goats.

As the "Mom and Pop Butcher Shop" of the North Market since 1993, Cheryl and David offer the kind of personal attention that can only come from farmers who raise their livestock on pasture and control the animals from birth to market. They will trim and portion to your preference. And they love to talk – they'll tell you about cuts you're not familiar with and offer advice based on specific recipes. "We enjoy helping people, and seeing people expand their culinary horizons and be happy with what they've bought from us," says Cheryl.

# BLUES creek

**FARM** meats

Phil Gulis, executive chef at Plate, prepares a special-occasion dinner with Bluescreek Farm rib rack of grass-fed lamb, ultra-tender and more refined in flavor than any other cut. His Market-friendly preparation includes a delightful medley of local vegetables, dressed with a verjus vinaigrette (the pressed juice of unripened Sangiovese grapes).

# Grilled Garlic-Rubbed Rack of Lamb
## WITH WARM VEGETABLE SALAD

*makes 2 servings*

### THE MAIN DISH

| | |
|---|---|
| 1 | Bluescreek Farm lamb rack |
| | salt and pepper, to taste |
| 1 | clove garlic, minced |
| 1 | small sprig of rosemary, chopped |
| 1/4 | cup extra virgin olive oil |

**1.** Season the lamb rack with salt and pepper. Stir together the garlic, rosemary, and olive oil into a thick paste. Rub the rack with the paste and allow to sit for 30 minutes.

**2.** Pre-heat grill to medium. Place lamb on grill, cooking to desired temperature (internal temperature of 135° F. is medium-rare, 160° F. is well-done).

**3.** When the lamb is finished, place it on a cutting board to rest for 5 minutes. Then, using a sharp knife, slice into thin medallions, and divide over the vegetables on 2 dinner plates. Slowly spoon the dressing over the lamb and vegetables.

### THE VEGETABLES

| | |
|---|---|
| 1/2 | medium zucchini, cut into 1/4″ rounds |
| 1/2 | medium eggplant, cut into 1/4″ rounds |
| | extra virgin olive oil |
| | salt and pepper, to taste |
| 1 | English cucumber, diced |
| 1 | small shallot, diced |
| 1 | poblano pepper, diced |
| 1 | heirloom tomato, diced |
| 4 | English pea pods, shucked and blanched |
| 1/2 | medium eggplant, cut into 1/4″ rounds |
| 6 | large basil leaves, torn into pieces by hand |
| 8 | large leaves of Italian parsley, torn by hand |

Lightly dress the zucchini and eggplant with olive oil, season with salt and pepper, and grill until tender. Combine with remaining vegetables in a mixing bowl, and divide between 2 dinner plates.

### THE DRESSING

| | |
|---|---|
| 2 | tablespoons Sangiovese Verjus |
| 1 | tablespoon red wine vinegar |
| 1/4 | cup extra virgin olive oil |
| 1 | teaspoon honey |
| 1 | teaspoon Dijon mustard |
| 1 | lemon zest, to taste |
| | salt and pepper, to taste |

In a small bowl, whisk together all ingredients.

# Momma Seifert's MEATLOAF WITH BACON-INFUSED MASHED POTATOES

*makes 6 servings*

Beginning his culinary journey as a fourteen-year-old apprentice, Hubert Seifert refined his skills in the kitchens of Brenner's Park Hotel in Baden-Baden, Pierre Troisgros in Lyon, and L'Auberge de I'll in Alsace-Lorraine, before opening Spagio in Columbus. "Meatloaf conveys hominess and reminds us of sharing a meal with family," explains the master chef, who still makes the dish the way his mother taught him.

## THE POTATOES

| | |
|---|---|
| 8 | Yukon Gold potatoes, peeled and cut in half lengthwise |
| 1 | tablespoon kosher salt + additional to taste |
| 2 | sticks cold unsalted butter (1/2 pound), diced |
| | pinch freshly-grated nutmeg |
| 1 1/2 | cups half & half |
| 8 | strips bacon, julienned and sautéed |

1. In a large stock pot add Yukon Gold potatoes, 1 tablespoon of salt and cover with cold water. Bring to a boil and simmer until "fork tender." Drain using a sieve, but do not rinse. Return potatoes to the pot and allow to "dry" over heat for 1 to 2 minutes. Add butter and nutmeg.

2. In a small sauce pan bring half & half to near scalding point. Add to the potato pot. Mash potato mixture to desired consistency. Season to taste. Either blend in sautéed bacon or sprinkle on top. Keep warm until ready to serve.

## THE MEATLOAF

| | |
|---|---|
| 1/2 | French baguette, cubed |
| 1 | pound each: ground veal, ground pork, and ground beef |
| 3 | large eggs, lightly whisked |
| 2 | tablespoons Dijon mustard |
| 4 | tablespoons Worcestershire sauce |
| 2 | tablespoons kosher salt |
| 2 | teaspoons black pepper, freshly-cracked |
| 1/4 | cup Italian parsley, finely-chopped |
| | food release spray, such as olive or canola oil |
| 1 | pound applewood-smoked bacon slices |

1. Preheat oven to 350° F. In a large bowl, soak baguette in cold water until just soft. Strain, squeezing out excess water.

2. In another large bowl, add ground veal, pork, beef, eggs, mustard, Worcestershire, baguette (soaked and strained), chopped parsley, salt, and 1 tablespoon of pepper. Hand mix well.

3. Coat a 9"x 13" pyrex or other heat-safe baking pan with non-stick food release spray. Lay strips of bacon to cover bottom and partial sides of pan. Press meat mixture into pan, making sure to remove any air pockets. Lay remaining bacon on top and sprinkle with 1 teaspoon of pepper. Bake in oven on a sheet pan (to prevent burning) until clear juices begin to flow, about 1 hour (to 180° F. internal temperature).

4. When done, remove the meatloaf from the pan and place on a large platter. Let rest for 10 minutes before slicing. Serve on warmed dinner plates along with mashed potatoes, passed family-style around the table.

A Northern Italian specialty, Osso Bucco ("bone with a hole") is made with the lower part of the leg surrounded by delicious robust meat. While the dish is more traditionally made with veal shanks, Chef Jamie George of Z Cucina di Spirito prepares his rendition with Bluescreek pork shanks. It's rich and delicious and served alongside root vegetables from Toad Hill Farm, bathed and roasted in Chianti.

# Pork Osso Bucco
*makes 4 servings*
## WITH CHIANTI-ROASTED ROOT VEGETABLES

### THE OSSO BUCCO

| | |
|---|---|
| 4 | pork shanks |
| | salt and pepper, to taste |
| 4 | tablespoons olive oil |
| 2 | medium onions, finely-diced |
| 2 | medium carrots, diced |
| 2 | celery stalks, diced |
| 3 | cloves garlic, crushed |
| 1 | teaspoon sage leaves, shredded |
| 1 | teaspoon chili flakes |
| 1 | cup dry white wine |
| 1 | cup chicken stock |
| | finely-chopped flat leaf parsley, for garnish |

1. Season the shanks generously with salt and pepper. Once seasoned, heat the oil and brown the shanks to a deep golden brown on both sides in a roasting pan large enough to hold the shanks in a single layer. Remove the shanks from the pan and keep warm.

2. Add the onions, carrots, celery, garlic, sage, and chili flakes to the pan and cook until the onion is translucent. Return the shanks to the pan, pour over the stock and wine. Scrape the base of the pan to remove the cooking residue. Bring to a strong simmer, cover the pan and cook over a moderate-low heat for 2½ to 3 hours, until fork tender.

4. Remove from the heat, distribute shanks among 4 warmed plates. Scatter chopped parsley over the top of each. Serve with a bowl of the root vegetables passed around the table family-style.

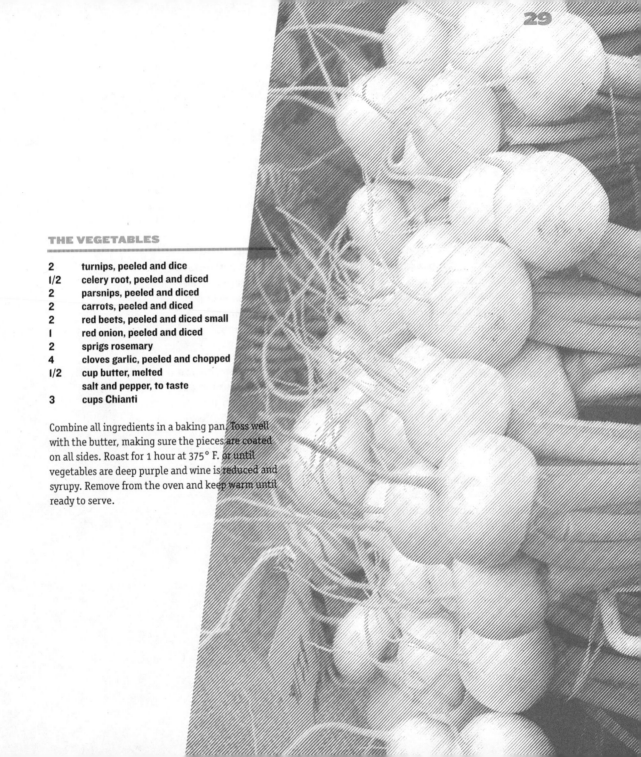

## THE VEGETABLES

| | |
|---|---|
| 2 | turnips, peeled and dice |
| 1/2 | celery root, peeled and diced |
| 2 | parsnips, peeled and diced |
| 2 | carrots, peeled and diced |
| 2 | red beets, peeled and diced small |
| 1 | red onion, peeled and diced |
| 2 | sprigs rosemary |
| 4 | cloves garlic, peeled and chopped |
| 1/2 | cup butter, melted |
| | salt and pepper, to taste |
| 3 | cups Chianti |

Combine all ingredients in a baking pan. Toss well
with the butter, making sure the pieces are coated
on all sides. Roast for 1 hour at 375° F. or until
vegetables are deep purple and wine is reduced and
syrupy. Remove from the oven and keep warm until
ready to serve.

# brēzel

**History gives the nod** to the German state of Bavaria, where the pretzel (or brēzel) was perfected and where the hearty, doughy twists of bravado are found in every local bakery and in countless beer gardens.

From its early roots, the pretzel was regarded as having religious significance. According to historians, its shape resembled the way early Christians prayed with arms folded across their chests, each hand on the opposite shoulder. Monks baked pretzels to reward children for reciting their prayers.

Pretzel baking has most firmly taken root at the North Market courtesy of an energetic young woman by the name of Brittany Baum, whose culinary awakening during visits to Germany inspired the launch of a modest baking enterprise in 2008, introducing Columbus to the authentic, Bavarian-style pretzel experience.

The big, beautiful pretzels are made from scratch every day at the Market, formed by hand as has been done for many generations. First, the dough needs to be rolled out. Both ends of the strand are held up, and through a quick swing, the center of the strand is twisted. The ends are then pressed onto the body of the pretzel. "The process takes only a few seconds," explains Brittany, "but it needs a lot of practice to get it right."

And, oh boy, once you catch a whiff of the biscuity aroma, all you can think of is getting your hands on one of those fresh-from-the-oven treats. The "original" Brēzel pretzel has a dark brown, crispy outside, studded with kosher salt, and a distinctively soft and supple texture on the inside, so genuinely German, you'll think you've been transported to Deutschland after just one bite. Sliced horizontally and buttered, it becomes a Butterbrēzel, or split and stuffed with slices of cold cuts, it's a meal unto itself

Locally-distilled Watershed Bourbon has many fans across the city, and Chef Marcus Andrew Meacham of Bodega is one of them. The slightly-sweet spirit becomes the base of a dip for the Brēzel pretzels served as bar snacks at the Short North eatery. Wash it all down with Elevator Brewing Company's "Horny Goat," a bourbon-barrel-aged porter with dark roast flavors and sweet vanilla and bourbon notes – a cooling contrast to the spicy dip.

# BODEGA "Whiskey Dip"

*makes 3 cups*

## THE DIP

| | |
|---|---|
| 3/4 | cup Watershed Bourbon |
| 1 | pound butter, cubed |
| 3/4 | cup brown sugar |
| 4 | teaspoons garlic powder |
| 2 | teaspoons cayenne pepper |

1. In a sauce pan, heat the bourbon until it begins to give off vapor. Carefully ignite the bourbon vapor and allow the flame to burn until it burns itself out (this cooks off the alcohol).

2. Stir in the butter cubes until melted. Add the brown sugar, garlic powder and cayenne pepper and stir until dissolved into the butter/bourbon mixture. Bring the dip to a boil and remove from the heat. Cool until a thick sauce is formed. Using an electric mixer or whisk, whip until fluffy.

3. Serve with assorted pretzels for dipping.

# Fonduta di Piemonte

*makes 3 cups*

Fontina cheese originates from the Italian Alps where a specific breed of cows is raised and milked to produce the creamy milk for this mild, somewhat nutty, herbaceous and fruity cheese. The soft texture of young Fontina melts beautifully in this Piedmontese version of fondue, perfect for pretzel-dipping from a community pot set in the center of the table. Enjoy with a bottle of bright, fruity Firelands Pinot Grigio. (Rubbing garlic inside the pot adds a little extra flavor to the fondue).

## THE DIP

| | |
|---|---|
| 1 | garlic clove, peeled |
| 16 | ounces Italian Fontina cheese, cut into 1/2" cubes |
| 1/2 | cup milk |
| 1/2 | cup heavy cream |
| 6 | tablespoons unsalted butter |
| 4 | egg yolks |
| | sea salt |
| | white pepper |

1. Rub the inside of the fondue pot with the garlic clove. Discard the garlic.

2. In a large saucepan, combine the cheese, milk and cream, and simmer over moderate heat, stirring continuously, until the cheese begins to melt, about 4 to 5 minutes. Whisk in the butter and egg yolks and continue stirring over low heat until very smooth. Remove from the heat and season with salt and pepper to taste.

3. Transfer the mixture to the warm fondue pot. Serve immediately with assorted pretzels for dipping.

**"My approach is to combine the old and new,"** says tea-barista and blender-jockey Eric Ling, who applies that strategy to the menu of concoctions he and his staff create at Bubbles, the Tea and Juice Company.

A native of Taiwan, Eric arrived in Columbus at age nineteen to study computer science and business at OSU. "The science degree was in order to keep my family happy," he explains, "and the business degree was to keep myself happy." He found gainful employment as an IT consultant, but it wasn't long before the ambitious young man succumbed to his passion for business and became an entrepreneur.

Time-honored tea culture of his homeland provided the inspiration for Eric's venture at the Market. Traditional teahouses or "tea-arts" shops are common throughout the country, and Eric wanted to re-create a place where tea lovers could meet and share a brew. His selection includes as many as two dozen green and black teas – calming and relaxing, energizing or soothing.

# bubbles
## THE TEA & JUICE COMPANY

It was also in Taiwan that a new tea drink originated – a sweet indulgence that gives the enterprise its name. Bubble Tea is a frothy, tea-based beverage combined with milk or fruit flavors and laden with bubble-like tapioca pearls which are sucked up through fat straws, providing a chewy contrast to the sweetness and texture of the drink. They are made to order, shaken the same way a bartender shakes a cocktail, and served on the rocks. "For the first-timers," says Eric, "ordering Bubble Tea can be an event."

Wildly popular though his teas and bubble teas are, Eric and his team have not rested on their laurels. In addition to a menu of creative smoothies, you can use your imagination to create your own blended beverage with almost endless possibilities of naturally sweet and creamy, Market-inspired combinations. Drink to your health!

# "Old Wives' Tale" HOT TODDY

*makes 1 drink*

Some folks claim a Hot Toddy at bedtime will relieve symptoms of the common cold or flu, but Cris Delhavi of Middle West Spirits thinks of it as a warming pick-me-up any time of the day or night during the cold winter months. Her confident formula calls for whiskey made with 100% red Ohio wheat, local honey, a squeeze of fresh lemon, and vanilla-infused tea from Bubbles. "Robust black tea is blended with warm, fragrant vanilla," explains Eric. "There is a comfort in the scent of vanilla that few other things can provide."

## COCKTAIL

| | |
|---|---|
| 1 | ounce OYO Whiskey |
| 1 | tablespoon "Fall Harvest" honey |
| 1/4 | ounce lemon juice, freshly-squeezed |
| 1 | cup water |
| 1 | heaping teaspoon Vanilla Black Tea leaves |
| | lemon wheel, thinly-sliced, for garnish |

**1.** Coat the bottom of a handled mug glass with honey. Add the whiskey and lemon juice.

**2.** Add tea leaves to a teapot. Bring water to a boil, pour into a teapot, and allow steeping for about three to five-minutes, and no longer.

**3.** Pour the steaming tea into the mug and stir. Float the lemon wheel on the surface of the drink and serve.

# THE Dave

*makes 1 serving*

Eric emphasizes deliciousness and balance in his drinks, and here's a mighty fine excuse for some sipping. Using mostly local ingredients for this creamy smoothie, he puts a clever spin on a soda-shop standard. Healthy, convenient and portable, "The Dave" is ideal for a quick breakfast, an afternoon snack, or an anytime fuel-on-the-go.

## DRINK

| | |
|---|---|
| 1 | banana |
| 1/8 | cup Krema "Natural Crunchy" peanut butter |
| 1/2 | cup Snowville Creamery or other fat-free milk |
| 1/2 | cup cracked ice |
| 2 | tablespoons Honeyrun Farm "Fall Harvest" |

In a blender, combine banana, peanut butter and milk. Blend until smooth and frothy. Pour into a tall glass and drizzle with honey. Serve immediately.

**Some like it hot** – and John Hard practices what he preaches. You might also say that dealing in heat comes naturally to John, a fire protection engineer who is enjoying a second act in the fiery foods business.

# CaJOHN'S flavor & fire

When work regularly took the Columbus native to the Gulf Coast region, he was captivated by the spicy local dishes, and was, in his words, "intrigued by what hurt." As an engineer, he wanted to understand how it worked – why once the burning sensation subsides, the pleasure remains. He read everything he could find about "heat" in foods and cultures that use the most spices. He began experimenting in his home kitchen, and set out to make the consummate hot sauce.

John's first batches of cayenne-garlic and habanero-garlic sauces really packed a punch, and with encouragement from family, he started bottling them up for sale. They were labeled "Hot Spots" after his two Dalmatians, Sparky and Blaze, at the suggestion of daughter Erin, and a new business venture was born.

The CaJohn's Flavor & Fire enterprise remained a sideline until 2004 when John sold the family's fire equipment company and became a full-time "saucier." Since then he has developed, produced and marketed an ambitious line of salsas, hot sauces, barbecue sauces, rubs, and seasonings in styles that range from mild to painfully hot. And speaking of pain, hardcore devotees can't seem to get enough of CaJohn's "Black Mamba," unapologetically derived from habañero peppers and capsaicin extracts. More common are products that show off the flavor as well as the heat of the ingredients.

John's dizzying display at the Market includes nearly 150 different concoctions. He and his staff educate customers regarding taste, flavor intensity, ingredients, and heat levels. "Matching hot sauces to foods is an art form," explains the man who has been burning his way into our hearts and stomachs for more than a decade.

"A freshly fried oyster is a thing to savor," says Chef Joshua Harris of Smith & Wollensky. "The crunchy coating is a welcome contrast to the soft, juicy oyster meat inside." The chef puts CaJohn's garlic and cayenne-based condiment to good use in a Buffalo-style partnership of hot sauce and bleu cheese – the heat and its cooling counterbalance – in a plate of oysters.

# Buffalo Fried Oysters
## WITH CRUMBLED BLEU CHEESE

*makes 4 servings*

### MAIN DISH

| | |
|---|---|
| | rock salt, to hold oyster shells in place |
| 2 | dozen oysters, shucked and drained, half-shells reserved |
| | shredded iceberg lettuce, as needed |
| 3/4 | cup all-purpose flour |
| | salt |
| | black pepper, freshly-cracked |
| | oil, for deep frying |
| 1/2 | cup bleu cheese dressing |
| 1/2 | cup CaJohn's Lil' Kick Louisiana Style Hot Sauce |
| 1/2 | cup bleu cheese dressing |
| | crumbled bleu cheese, for garnish |
| | chopped fresh parsley, for garnish |

**1.** Prepare 4 dishes with coarse salt to keep 6 oyster half-shells upright, and fill each shell with a portion of the shredded lettuce. Set aside.

**2.** Mix the flour with salt and pepper to taste. Dredge the oysters in the seasoned flour. Deep fry in batches in oil heated to 375° F. and fry until golden brown, about 2 minutes. Drain briefly on paper towels, then toss in the hot sauce.

**3.** Add 1 teaspoon of the bleu cheese dressing onto each lettuce-filled shell, then place a dressed oyster on top; sprinkle with crumbled bleu cheese and parsley. Serve at once, passing any extra hot sauce alongside.

# Le Chou Rouge Braisé

*makes 4 servings*

A head of red cabbage becomes a tasty, Cajun-inspired side dish in which apples offer a tart retort to CaJohn's Hot Spots "Fireball." The equilibrium between the sweet, sour, and spicy flavors provides splendid accompaniment to venison, goose or pork. To build a full dinner around it, serve with some good rye bread, a wedge of cheddar cheese, or perhaps a soft blue.

## SIDE DISH

| | |
|---|---|
| 1 | large onion, chopped |
| 1/4 | cup butter |
| 1/2 | cup dry red wine |
| 1/4 | cup packed brown sugar |
| 1/4 | cup apple cider vinegar |
| 1 | teaspoon minced garlic |
| 1 | tart apple, peeled, cored and roughly-chopped |
| 1 | head of red cabbage, quartered, cut crosswise into 1/2" strips |
| | Hot Spots "Fireball" or other hot sauce |

1. Sauté the onions in the butter in a large, lidded skillet over medium heat until clear. Add the wine, sugar, vinegar, and garlic, stir and let simmer for 3 minutes. Add the apple and simmer uncovered until the apple is tender, about 2 to 3 minutes.

2. Add the cabbage, toss to coat thoroughly, then cover the pot and cook over low heat for 45 minutes, stirring from time to time. Remove from heat and season with hot sauce as desired.

3. To serve, transfer to a warmed serving bowl, and pass family-style around the table.

**There are plenty of cheeses to choose from** in a typical supermarket, but at the North Market you can have a one-on-one discussion with an expert who will guide you through an impressive and varied selection to a cheese that suits your taste or pairs with the wines and foods you've chosen for your meal. In the tradition of a Parisian fromager, he'll tell you about each of the cheeses, what makes them special, what's best at the moment – and he'll encourage you to taste before you buy!

The self-proclaimed cheesemonger is Mike Kast, whose curious palate developed during his youth in the serious food town of Chicago. When he arrived in Columbus, courtesy of a military transfer, he became a regular shopper at the North Market, and after a stint at The Limited, went to work for Ed Malzone, the Market's cheese vendor. The more he learned, the greater his desire to "monger" cheese, and in 1988 he purchased Ed's business and established Curds & Whey.

"Just inhaling the funky, pungent aromas is like heaven to me," says Mike, who is surrounded by "cheesy comestibles" in every direction. He offers a rotating selection of handmade offerings, and as is the practice in all good cheese shops, his wheels and blocks are hand-cut to order for your joyful consumption.

Mike is an advocate for Ohio-made, artisanal and farmhouse cheeses, and he keeps close contacts with local producers. "People are looking for cheeses they can't easily find in the grocery store," he explains, "and our local producers are creating interesting varieties." He singles out the artisan goat's milk cheeses of Lake Erie Creamery, a small urban creamery in Cleveland, and Kokoborrego farmstead sheep milk cheese from Sippel Family Farm in Mount Gilead. "There's a lot of good cheese in our own backyard."

The visit to a cheese shop can be a daunting experience, but not at Curds and Whey, thanks to Mike Kast. As more people are asking questions about where their food comes from, the personalized service served up at his cheese counter helps to provide answers.

CURDS & whey

# Ploughman's Lunch

*makes 4 servings*

In the early 1800s, British wives sent their husbands off to plough the fields with a packed lunch, thereafter inspiring simple cold plates in country pubs which might include a thick chunk of local cheese, a mainplate salad, loaf of crusty bread, radishes and scallions or fresh fruit, perhaps an apple or a bunch of grapes. The possibilities for other components are many. Mike recommends "Miami Erie Canal," nutty with a sweet note, Emmentaler or Swiss-style cheese from Canal Junction Farmstead in Defiance County. To complete the local theme, serve with easy-sipping Wyandotte Winery "Great Southern," made from Ohio Seyval Blanc grapes.

## MAIN DISH

| | |
|---|---|
| 1/2 | cup extra-virgin olive oil, plus extra for skillet |
| 2 | tablespoons red wine vinegar |
| | salt |
| | black pepper, freshly-cracked |
| 8 | prosciutto slices, cut into small squares |
| 2 | garlic cloves, minced |
| 1 | handful romaine |
| 1 | handful radicchio |
| 1 | handful watercress |
| 1 | handful mizuna |
| 4 | wedges Canal Junction Farmstead "Miami Erie Canal" |
| 8 | radishes, with tops intact |
| 8 | scallion leaves |

In a large bowl, whisk together the oil, vinegar, salt and pepper to taste. In an oiled skillet, cook the prosciutto over moderate-high heat, stirring, until browned, about 5 minutes. Add the garlic and continue stirring, about 1 minute. Add the vinaigrette and stir to combine. Allow to cool slightly.

2. Pour the warm dressing into a large bowl, add the greens, mix and gently toss to coat evenly.

3. To assemble the salad, set out 4 chilled serving plates. Divide the dressed greens among the plates. Add a generous wedge of cheese, 2 radishes, and 2 scallion leaves to each serving. Serve with crusty bread.

# LOADED POTATO CHIPS
## with gorgonzola-parmesan-garlic sauce
# FOR *"The Cheese Man"*

*makes 8–10 servings*

According to Mario Batali, "Gorgonzola is indisputably one of Italy's greatest contributions to the world." A youthful gorgonzola is moist and soft, almost creamy, with buttery, piquant flavor and a long, lingering finish. Its subtle nuttiness blends perfectly with parmesan and garlic in a savory topping for crunchy, house-made potato chips by Chef Ed Straight of Local Roots.

## THE SAUCE

| | |
|---|---|
| 2 | teaspoons corn starch |
| 2 | pints heavy cream |
| 1/4 | cup chopped fresh garlic |
| 2 | cups crumbled gorgonzola cheese |
| 2 | cups shredded parmesan cheese |

Mix the corn starch with the heavy cream and garlic and heat in a large sauce pan over low heat. Do not burn. When cream begins to simmer, whisk in Parmesan cheese until fully melted, and continue whisking until thickened. Remove from the heat and keep warm until needed.

## THE CHIPS

| | |
|---|---|
| 6 – 8 | Yukon Gold potatoes, sliced into 1/8" slices on a mandolin or other handheld slicer |
| | peanut oil, for frying |
| | salt |
| | cheese sauce (from left) |
| 6 | slices bacon, cooked and diced |
| 1 | bunch fresh green onions, diced |

**1.** In a large heavy saucepan, fill oil no more than halfway, and heat the oil to 350° F. Add the potato slices in batches. Fry until light golden brown, about 2 to 3 minutes. Drain on paper towels and season with salt immediately.

**2.** To serve, transfer chips to a large platter, drizzle the cheese sauce over the chips, and sprinkle bacon and green onions over the top.

# Parmesan Crème Brûlée
## with caramelized rosemary-sugar crust

*makes 8 servings*

At Basi Italia, Chef John Dornback takes a classic Italian dessert and deftly recasts it into a dish with savory swagger. Heavy cream mingles with parmesan cheese and eggs to create a silky, smooth custard that contrasts with a thin, crisp layer of rosemary-infused caramel – a balance of creamy and crisp, sweet and bitter, light and deep. (If a hand-held torch in unavailable, caramelize the sugar on the top rack of the broiler, watching the custards carefully to be sure the sugar doesn't burn). The brûlée can be baked a day in advance and refrigerated. Bring to room temperature, then finish with the caramel just before serving.

### THE BRÛLÉE

| | |
|---|---|
| 1 | quart heavy cream |
| 2 | cups grated parmesan cheese |
| 1/4 | cup sugar |
| 1 | bay leaf |
| 12 | egg yolks, at room temperature |
| | rosemary sugar (from below) |

### THE ROSEMARY SUGAR

| | |
|---|---|
| 1/4 | cup sugar |
| 1/4 | cup fresh rosemary leaves |

Combine sugar and rosemary leaves in a food processer and mix until fine. Set aside until ready to use.

1. In a heavy pot bring heavy cream to a boil. Reduce heat to a simmer and add parmesan, sugar, and bay leaf. Mix well. Reduce heat further to low and stir regularly, about 5 minutes (the cheese will burn at this stage if not stirred). Remove pan from heat and let mixture stand in a warm place for 10 minutes. Strain mixture and reserve.

2. In a large bowl mix egg yolks thoroughly. While the strained cream mixture is still warm, wisk into the egg yolks a little at a time, until thoughly incorporated.

3. Divide mixture into eight 4-ounce ramekins. Arrange ramekins in a high-sided baking pan and fill baking pan with enough hot water to reach halfway up the sides of the ramekins. Carefully place pan into a 350° oven for 20 to 25 minutes (or until custard is set in the center). Remove pan from oven and let custards cool in water bath. Carefully remove custards from water bath, cover each ramekin with foil or plastic wrap and chill for at least 2 hours.

4. When ready to serve, remove plastic wrap or foil and sprinkle each custard with 2 teaspoons of the rosemary sugar. Use a hand-held torch to caramelize the sugar quickly, allowing the sugar to harden.

# EXPRESSLY MARKET BAKERY AND BISTRO

**With fond childhood memories of the North Market,** best friends Gay James and Luann Riley set out to create what they had always envisioned: a community-friendly eatery with the freshest ingredients, a variety of choices to create healthy sandwiches and salads, flavorful homemade soups, and made-from-scratch sweets ranging from cookies and cakes to fat pies. These are foods that taste good and are good for you, all invitingly displayed at Expressly Market Bakery and Bistro.

The two women describe their partnership as a balance between the creative and the practical, the savory and the sweet. With Gay on the food front and Luann in charge behind the scenes, they are on a mutual mission, and the passion in their work is obvious. "The food we serve represents the way we like to eat," explains Gay. "It's honest food with flavor and texture. That's really important to us."

Soup offerings change with the seasons – choices include Pumpkin Chili in the Fall, Split Pea and Black Bean Gumbo in Winter, and Gazpacho in Spring and Summer. To the delight of vegetarians, salads are abundant with local and organic bounty whenever available. Sandwiches are quick and portable, served on breads and Kaiser rolls from family-owned Schwebel

Bakery. Egg Salad, Chicken Salad, Italian-style Hummus, and the "CLT" (cucumber, lettuce, tomato, with herbed cream cheese) keep customers coming back for more.

And be sure to leave room for one of the delectable desserts. Treat yourself to chocolate cake, carrot cake, cookies, and "no-bakes," those chewy treats that date back to home kitchens in the 1950s. "It's one of the first things I learned to make when I was a kid," says Luann.

Eat in or take home dinner options are prepared with health in mind but with all the flavors we crave. This is a place where everyone can feel welcome and customers become regulars. "Our staff knows many of them by name," says Gay, "and that's the way we like it."

# "After School" COOKIE PLATE

*makes 2-3 dozen cookies*

Should you be unable to find a cookie-laden Girl Scout in your neighborhood, Gay and Luann offer a cuddly assortment, not just for kids, but for kid in all of us. Set out as an after-school snack. Or serve as an unexpected dessert course at an adult dinner party with coffee and cordials as the main course is cleared. The signature Expressly-style cookies are mostly egg-free and dairy-free but so yummy you'd never guess they're good for you.

## THE LEMON BARS

### CRUST
| | |
|---|---|
| 1 1/2 | cups flour |
| 1/2 | cup powdered sugar |
| 3/4 | cup butter (softened) |

Combine crust ingredients together until crumbly. Press evenly into the bottom of a greased 9" x 13" cake pan. Bake for 15 minutes at 350° F.

### TOPPING
| | |
|---|---|
| 1 1/2 | cups sugar |
| 1/4 | cup flour |
| 4 | eggs |
| 8 | tablespoons freshly-squeezed lemon juice |
| 2 | tablespoons lemon zest |
| 2 | teaspoons baking powder (non-aluminum) |
| 1/2 | teaspoon salt |

Beat together the topping ingredients until frothy. Pour topping over pre-baked crust. Return to the 350° F. oven and bake until top is firm and lightly brown, about 25 minutes.

## THE CASHEW BARS

### CRUST
1 1/2   cups flour
6        ounces margarine
1/2      cup dark brown sugar

Mix together until crumbly. Grease a 9" x 13" cake pan.
Press crust mixture evenly into bottom of cake pan.
Bake for 15 minutes at 350° F.

### TOPPING
3/4     cup margarine
1       cup dark brown sugar
1/2     teaspoon salt
2       egg replacers (Ener-g)
2       teaspoons vanilla extract
1       tablespoon soy milk
1 1/2   cups lightly-salted cashews
1 1/2   cups carob chips

1.  Add margarine and brown sugar into a saucepan
and stir constantly over medium heat until the sugar
and margarine are melted together and start to
thicken.

2.  In a separate bowl, mix together salt, egg
replacers, vanilla, and soy milk. When the caramel
is done, combine together.

3.  When crust is finished pre-baking, fill with liquid
mixture. Sprinkle the cashews and carob chips on top.
Bake in a 350° F. oven until bubbly on top, about 25
minutes. Remove from the oven; allow to cool and firm
up. (It is easiest to cut when still just a little warm).

## THE DOUBLE CHOCOLATE CHIP COOKIES

3/4     cup canola or other vegetable oil
2       cups sugar
2       teaspoons vanilla extract
1/2     cup soy milk
2       cups flour
3/4     cup cocoa
1       teaspoon baking soda
1/2     teaspoon salt
1       cup chocolate chips (vegan)
1       egg replacer (Ener-g)

Combine all ingredients in a large mixing bowl (dough
will be a bit sticky). Spoon dough onto parchment lined
cookie trays. Bake for 9 to 10 minutes at 350° F.

# FIRDOUS express

**Growing up in a home where food was important,** Abdul Aburmaieleh's childhood may have been the perfect preparation for running a Middle Eastern eatery. "Both my parents were very good cooks," he explains. "Food is life in a Jordanian household and sharing it is one of the greatest joys." Recollections of his homeland include a family kitchen that was always filled with platters of food.

Upon arrival in the United States at age twenty, Abdul settled in Columbus and quickly delved into cooking. He began working for Nasir Latif, the Palestinian owner of Firdous Express, at that time located on High Street near the OSU campus. There, he discovered his passion for sharing the culture and cuisine of his youth. After stints in law enforcement and competitive body-building, he returned to his culinary calling, purchased Firdous Express, and re-dedicated himself to the Middle Eastern kitchen at the Market.

While focusing on the purest, most authentic versions of the foods of his native Jordan, the full menu encompasses a culinary sampler from a range of Mediterranean cuisines. If Abdul and his adventurous Algerian chef, Kamal Afafsa, can't convert you into a lover of foods with heady spices that give each dish an extraordinary fragrance and depth of flavor, than no one can. "We love flavors that surprise you," says Abdul. "Not things that are too crazy, but that create contrast in the mouth."

Bread is an essential ingredient and all dishes are served with a pita pocket for picking up meat, vegetables, and salads and as a scoop for sauces and dips.

The name "Firdous" was inspired by the ancient Persian legend of a bountiful garden, appropriate to a venture that honors the cuisines evolved over centuries of cultural interaction and provides a savory oasis at the Market.

# TUNISIAN Chicken Stew

*makes 4 servings*

Sharing a meal with others is a treasured tradition in Arabic regions, an expression of hospitality. If you are the host, you say *tafathalo*, which means "do me the honor," a gracious invitation to the table. It is said that a husband can judge his wife's affections by the amount of hot peppers she uses when preparing his food. If the food becomes bland then a man may believe that his wife no longer loves him. Note to wives: When preparing this traditional Middle Eastern stew, adjust seasonings accordingly.

## MAIN DISH

| | |
|---|---|
| 3 | tablespoons olive oil |
| 2 | onions, peeled and finely-chopped |
| 6 | garlic cloves, minced |
| 1 | tablespoon paprika |
| 1 | teaspoon crushed red pepper |
| 1/2 | teaspoon cayenne pepper |
| 4 | skinless, boneless chicken breasts, cut into 1" cubes |
| 4 | cups low-sodium chicken broth |
| 1/4 | cup coriander powder |
| 1 | tablespoon caraway seeds |
| 2 | cups diced carrots |
| 2 | cups diced celery |
| 1 | (6-ounce) can tomato paste |
| 1 | (16-ounce) can chopped tomatoes, undrained |
| 2 | cups diced zucchini |
| 1 | (15-ounce) can chickpeas, drained |
| 1 | cup black olives, pitted |
| | salt |
| | black pepper, freshly-cracked |
| | cooked couscous |
| | chopped fresh parsley, for garnish |

1. Heat oil in a large heavy pot over medium-high heat. Add onions and sauté until tender and starting to caramelize, about 8 minutes. Stir in garlic, paprika, red pepper, and cayenne, and cook until fragrant, about 1 minute.

2. Add the chicken and sauté for 1 minute. Add broth, coriander powder, caraway seeds, carrots, celery, tomato paste, and tomatoes, and bring to a boil. Reduce heat to medium; stir in zucchini, chick peas, and olives; simmer until chicken is just cooked through, about 15 minutes. Season with salt and pepper to taste.

3. Remove stew from the heat, transfer to a warmed serving bowl, and garnish with the chopped parsley. Serve from the bowl, passing a bowl of couscous alongside.

the FISH

**Seekers of the freshest seafood** in town need look no further than the well-trafficked counter operated by The Fish Guys. Ever since Bob Reany, the original "Fish Guy" began offering fresh catch in 1995, the North Market has had a fishmonger of the highest order.

Almost as soon as he could walk, Doug Denny was out fishing with his family and eating the day's catch. He gave up a career in market research to work alongside the Fish Guy, and in 2006, Doug took over where Bob left off. From the marketing department to the Market, he's now at the helm of the city's "go to" place for a wide range of seafood and freshwater fish.

The reliability of a local merchant is of utmost importance, and regulars have come to trust Doug and his dedicated crew. "Deliveries arrive from East Coast markets everyday by air, then are trucked directly to us," he says. "It doesn't get any fresher unless you're catching it yourself." His mission includes shortening the time when fish is yanked from the sea to the moment it's on your dinner plate. He offers the means to keep products safe and fresh until customers can get them home. If you visit his booth and have forgotten to bring your cooler or insulated bag, he offers baggies of ice. He'll clean fish for you at no extra charge, so you need not worry about having to clean them yourself.

Building a loyal following requires educating customers. The Fish Guys know how to handle, store, present and care for the seafood they sell – and it shows. Not only can you learn where your fish comes from, but they can tell you how to prepare and cook it too. They'll show you how to shuck an oyster or clam or explain how to properly prepare a lobster.

You can tell that Doug is passionate about what he does, and his Market stand is a seafood buyer's dream. We may be landlocked in Columbus, but it's never been easier to eat as well as a pescatarian.

GUYS

# PAN-FRIED LAKE ERIE WALLEYE
## with Peppered Shallot Cream Sauce

*makes 4 servings*

During the early spring, Walleye migrate to the spawning streams just off of Lake Erie, particularly the Maumee River basin in western Ohio. During the remainder of the year, these medium-size freshwater fish are caught in the deep waters of the lake. Chef Jeff Lindemeyer of Cameron's American Bistro has mastered the preparation of this regional favorite, brightened with a shallot cream sauce.

## THE CREAM SAUCE

| | |
|---|---|
| 1/2 | teaspoon black pepper, freshly-cracked |
| 1/4 | cup quarter-diced chopped shallots |
| 1/2 | cup white wine |
| 1/4 | cup clam juice |
| 2 | cups heavy cream |
| 1/2 | teaspoon minced garlic |
| 1/2 | teaspoon Tabasco |
| | cornstarch slurry, as needed |
| 4 | teaspoons lemon juice |
| | salt |

In a sauté pan, reduce wine and clam juice with pepper and shallots by half. Add heavy cream and bring to a simmer. Add garlic and slurry to thicken. Add Tabasco, lemon juice, and season with salt to taste. If making ahead, chill the finished sauce in an ice bath, refrigerate.

**NOTE** *Makes 2 ½ cups of sauce.*

## THE WALLEYE

| | |
|---|---|
| 4 | (6-ounce) Walleye filets |
| | salt |
| | black pepper, freshly-cracked |
| | all-purpose flour, as needed |
| | egg wash (1 egg + 2 tablespoons milk), as needed |
| | Ritz Cracker crumbs, as needed |
| | olive oil |
| | shallot cream sauce (from left) |
| | scallions, thinly-sliced, for garnish |

1. Season Walleye with salt and pepper to taste. Bread with flour and egg wash, then Ritz Cracker crumbs. Heat a cast iron (or non-stick) frying pan, add a splash of olive oil and place the fish fillets into the pan. Cook just until the filets flake when touched with a fork. (Walleye is a delicate fish and care should be taken not to overcook).

2. To serve, add a pool of the cream sauce to each of 4 warmed dinner plates. Top each with a filet, and garnish with the scallions.

"That marvel of delicacy," writes Henry Ward Beecher, "that concentration of sapid excellence, that mouthful before all other mouthfuls." To a purist, anything that adorns a raw oyster is unloved, but for the less devout, Chef Kent Rigsby's creamy, spicy sauce compliments the succulent texture and taste of the sea.

# Oysters Diavolo

*makes 4 servings*

## MAIN DISH

| | |
|---|---|
| 1 | cup flour |
| | salt |
| | black pepper, freshly-cracked |
| 4 | 1/4" slices eggplant |
| 2 | eggs, beaten with a little water to make egg wash |
| 1 | cup breadcrumbs |
| | vegetable oil, for frying |
| 6 | ounces heavy cream |
| 16 | select oysters, shucked |
| 3 | teaspoons slice scallions |
| 3 | tablespoons chopped canned tomatoes |
| 3 | teaspoons Tabasco |

1. Season flour with ¼ teaspoon salt and a turn of pepper. Coat eggplant slices with flour, shaking off excess. Then dip in egg wash, lift out and press into breadcrumbs, making sure to coat all the eggplant slice with the breadcrumbs.

2. Heat oil in a large saucepan to 375° F. Fry the eggplant until golden brown, remove from the oil and drain on paper towels.

3. Heat a large skillet over medium-high heat. Add the heavy cream and bring to a boil. Let cook for about 30 seconds to slightly reduce, then add the oysters, scallions, tomatoes, and Tabasco. Season with salt and pepper to taste. Poach the oysters in the cream, stirring and turning over with a spoon. Cook for about 2 to 3 minutes, until the oysters start to plump up.

4. Place 1 eggplant slice on each of 4 warmed plates. Lift the oysters out of the sauce with a slotted spoon and place 4 oysters on each eggplant disk.

5. Reduce the sauce a slightly thickened consistency, then spoon a little of the reduced sauce over each oyster plate and serve immediately.

# flavors
## OF INDIA

**On a visit to the North Market** during the 2012 Presidential campaign, Vice President Joe Biden stopped by the Flavors of India counter. "He asked me about my background," explains proprietor Raj Brar, "and I learned that he has visited my native region of Punjab. It made me very happy."

It was in his Indian homeland where Raj had an early start for the career that he eventually would pursue. He studied hospitality and cooking, fine-tuning his taste buds from childhood meals with his close-knit family. "I grew up in a home where eating good food was a priority," he recalls.

Raj came to the U.S. in 1978 for a position with the Indian-owned Stars Group of hotels and restaurants in New York. Two years later, he was lured to Columbus by his brother, whose wife had started Flavors of India at the Market. Eventually, Raj and his wife Billan became sole owners of the enterprise.

Those were the days of the old Market, when vendors were still ensconced in the Quonset hut and the volume of business was unpredictable. Raj recalls one day when he was working alone and a long line of customers assembled at his stand. "I was taking orders at the counter, going back to prepare the food, returning to collect the money, then doing it all again – and again. It was the longest day of my life."

Indian food is characterized by the complex layering of spices, many of which contribute more than heat to a dish. Raj and Bilan don't just add spices to food; they consider how each spice will be used and what characteristic of it should be emphasized. "We treat the spices in ways that make each dish rich, delicious, and deeply satisfying," says Raj.

Marketgoers enjoy the passionately-crafted dishes by folks who are not only dedicated to cooking the best Indian foods, but also dedicated to spreading the hospitable culture of India.

# Mixed Vegetable KORMA

*makes 4 servings*

Korma is a very old style of curry which can be traced back to the food culture of the Moghuls in Northern India. "Don't be put off by the number of ingredients in this lovely dish," says Raj. It's rich and creamy, with syncopated layers of spice – mild but not bland. The vegetables should be cut into large enough pieces to give a substantial look and feel to the dish. Keep calm and curry on!

## MAIN DISH

| | |
|---|---|
| 1 1/2 | tablespoons vegetable oil |
| 1 | small onion, diced |
| 1 | teaspoon minced ginger |
| 4 | cloves garlic, minced |
| 2 | russet potatoes, peeled and cubed |
| 4 | carrots, cubed |
| 1 | jalapeño, seeded and sliced |
| 3 | tablespoons ground, unsalted cashews |
| 4 | ounces tomato sauce |
| 2 | teaspoons salt |
| 1 1/2 | tablespoons curry powder |
| 1 | cup frozen green peas |
| 1/2 | green bell pepper, chopped |
| 1 | cup heavy cream |
| | chopped fresh cilantro, for garnish |
| | basmati rice, cooked |

1. In a large oiled skillet over medium heat, add the onions and cook until tender. Add ginger and garlic and cook, about 1 to 2 minutes.

2. In a medium bowl, mix together potatoes, carrots, jalapeno, cashews and tomato sauce. Add salt and curry powder, and then add to skillet. Cook, stirring continuously, until potatoes are tender, about 10 minutes. Add green bell pepper and cream to the skillet. Reduce heat to low, cover and simmer 10 minutes.

3. Remove stew from the heat, transfer to a warmed serving bowl, and garnish with the chopped cilantro. Serve from the bowl, passing a bowl of basmati rice alongside.

Recreate the complex flavors, texture and colors of North India's cuisine with this much-beloved snack or street food from the state of Punjab. The addition of coriander (or dhaniya powder) adds a warm tone to the nutty, satisfying taste of chickpeas, while the aromas practically fling themselves at you. You may find yourself making the dish over and over again to achieve just the right amount of spice you like.

# Punjabi Chole

*makes 6 servings*

## MAIN DISH

| | |
|---|---|
| 2 | cups chickpeas |
| 1/2 | mint leaf |
| 1/2 | cup cilantro |
| 4 | medium tomatoes |
| 5 | cloves |
| 3 | cinnamon sticks |
| 3 | green chilies |
| 3 | russet potatoes |
| 5 | tablespoons oil |
| 1/2 | teaspoon mustard seeds |
| 1 | teaspoon cumin seeds |
| 1/2 | cup chopped onions |
| 1/2 | teaspoon coriander powder |
| 1/4 | teaspoon garam masala powder |
| 1/2 | teaspoon chole masala powder |
| | turmeric, to taste |
| | salt, to taste |
| | chili powder, to taste |
| 2 | lemons, cut into wedges |
| | chopped coriander leaves, for garnish |
| | basmati rice, cooked |

1. Soak chickpeas in water overnight, (water should be 2 inches above settled chickpeas). Once chickpeas have soaked, drain and transfer to a large cooking pot. Cover with water twice the amount of chickpeas and bring to a boil. Cover and allow to simmer for approximately one hour. Do a taste test at this point to make sure they are tender. Drain and allow to cool for 10 minutes.

2. In a blender, puree mint, cilantro, tomatoes, and green chilies.

3. Boil potatoes, then peel and cut into small cubes. Heat oil in in a deep skillet. Add mustard seeds, cumin seeds, cloves, cinnamon sticks, onions and turmeric powder. Fry until onions turn gold.

4. Add the previously set aside pureed mixture. Let simmer for a minute. Add coriander powder, garam masala powder, chole masala, tumeric, salt and chili powder. Cook until mixture thickens. Add half cup of water as needed and proceed to cook until gravy thickens.

5. Remove stew from the heat, discard the cinnamon sticks, transfer to a warmed serving bowl, and garnish with the coriander leaves. Serve from the bowl, passing a bowl of basmati rice and lemon wedges alongside.

# the GREENER grocer

**They make a good fit** in what Michael Jones refers to as "the tapestry of the Market." He and operations manager Colleen Yuhn encourage marketgoers to explore the richness of our local foods and connect with local food producers.

In early 2008, they began establishing relationships with central Ohio growers, creating a year-round farmer's market within the North Market. The Greener Grocer operates under the umbrella of Local Matters, whose mission includes educating children and adults about healthy food, where it comes from, how to grow it, and how to cook it. "Our presence at the Market has become an outreach point," explains Michael, "providing a reliable retail outlet and encouraging farmers to grow more healthy foods."

"With the high profile of a permanent stand at the Market, we promote the benefits of buying local," says Colleen. "We're passionate about our produce, and we love helping our customers get to know the hard-working men and women who grow it."

"We wanted to make eating local and regional food as easy and convenient as possible," says Michael, so we started a CSA (Community Supported Agriculture) program." The Greener Grocer Market Bag is packed with seasonal, fresh fruits and vegetables that support local, family farms on a year-round basis. You pay at the beginning of the growing season, and then, throughout both summer and winter subscription plans, you get to pick up a bag full of freshly-picked veggies once a week. You never know what you'll get until you open your bag.

"The Greener Grocer is a 'real time' expression of the overall philosophy in our nonprofit work," says Colleen, "and it provides us with a public face to put our beliefs into practice and have some fun conversations with folks at the Market. We're educating all day long!"

# WHOLE GRAIN RISOTTO
## with Shiitake Mushrooms and Kale

*makes 8 servings*

You'll need a heavy pan with a copper bottom for even distribution of heat and a wooden spoon for gently stirring. The grains not only add a wholesome nutritional dimension to the risotto, but delicious texture and appealing nutty flavor. Create a wonderful dinner party by preparing ingredients in advance, then having your guests take turns stirring.

### MAIN DISH

| | |
|---|---|
| 1 | pound local spelt or wheat berries (pre-cooked in 1-quart chicken or vegetable stock; cover and simmer 50 to 60 minutes until tender) |
| 2 | tablespoons olive oil |
| 1/2 | sweet onion, diced |
| 2 | cloves of garlic, minced |
| 1 | pound shiitake mushrooms, roasted & sliced thin |
| 1 | bunch of kale, blanched in boiling salted water & chopped |
| 1/2 | cup of Snowville heavy cream |
| | kosher salt |
| | black pepper, freshly-cracked |

1. In a large sauté pan, sauté the onion in the olive oil until soft. Add the garlic and mushrooms and warm. Add the greens and sauté briefly. Add the pre-cooked spelt or wheat berries and the heavy cream and simmer on low heat, stirring constantly, allowing the cream to be absorbed. Season with salt and pepper to taste.

2. Transfer risotto to a warmed casserole dish. Serve family-style around the table.

# "LOCAL ROOTS" Composed Salad

*makes 8 servings*

Inspired by Salade Niçoise from Nice, on the Mediterranean Sea, Chef Edward Straight of Local Roots in Powell puts a truly local spin on the composed salad, sourcing as many ingredients as possible from The Greener Grocer. Like its French cousin, the arranged, vegetable-centric salad takes some time to prepare, given all the components. This is one dish where setting up your *mise en place* (all ingredients chopped and ready to go) will help the salad come together artfully.

## THE SALAD

| | |
|---|---|
| 3 | carrots, chopped into 1/2" cubes |
| 3 | beets, chopped into 1/2" cubes |
| 3 | parsnips, chopped into 1/2" cubes |
| 1/2 | cup balsamic vinegar |
| | salt |
| | black pepper, freshly-cracked |
| 6 | redskin potatoes, quartered |
| 6 | eggs, hard-boiled and quartered |
| 3 | heirloom tomatoes, diced |
| 32 | ounces seasonal mixed greens |
| | red wine vinaigrette (from right) |

**1.** Mix together carrots, beets, and parsnips with enough balsamic vinegar to coat. Season with salt and pepper to taste. Roast on a well-oiled pan at 350° F. for 20 minutes. On a separate pan, roast quartered redskin potatoes at 350° F. for 20 minutes. Remove both pans from the oven and allow to cool. Transfer separately to covered containers and chill in the fridge until ready to use.

**2.** To prepare, arrange eggs, tomatoes, root vegetable mix, and potatoes in separate piles on 8 chilled serving plates and mound a bed of greens at the center of each. Just before serving, drizzle vinaigrette over the salad. Serve at once, passing any extra vinaigrette alongside.

## THE VINAIGRETTE

| | |
|---|---|
| 1 | cup red wine vinegar |
| 1 | shallot |
| 2 | teaspoons fresh garlic, diced |
| 2 | teaspoons Dijon mustard |
| 2 | tablespoons honey |
| 1 | tablespoon fresh basil |
| 1 | tablespoon fresh oregano |
| 1 | tablespoon fresh parsley |
| 2 | cups olive oil |
| | salt |
| | black pepper, freshly-cracked |

Add all ingredients except the olive oil to a blender.
With machine running slowly, gradually add olive
oil. Season with salt and pepper to taste. Chill the
vinaigrette for several hours or more.

# HEIL'S

# FAMILY deli

In 1954, Wayne Heil, an entrepreneur who ran an import-export business and a telephone answering service, began producing deli salads for grocery retailers around the state. By the 1960s he was the biggest supplier between New York and Chicago, churning out 10,000 pounds of potato salad, coleslaw, macaroni salad, and fruit salad every week.

In January of 1969, Wayne bought out the old-school North Market deli at the Quonset hut and put up his shingle as Heil's Family Deli. He began serving up meats and cheeses by the pound, making brawny sandwiches, homemade soups, and, of course, the secret-recipe potato salad on which he would build a longstanding reputation.

"He claimed they spilled more potato salad on the floor than most delis make all together," says Alex Kushkin, who left his podiatry practice to purchase the business when Wayne retired in 2000. Thankfully, little has changed in the meantime. The legacy lives on with the old-fashioned, made-by-hand potato salad, not one of those drippy wet ones that taste more like mayonnaise than potatoes. "We use fresh white potatoes,"

says Alex, "and we don't use fillers – or what I call 'schmutz.' You can eat an entire bowlful of the stuff and call it dinner."

Alex grew up in his family's deli in Akron, so he's no stranger to the crafting of sliced meats between two slices of bread to create a thing of beauty. He brings joy and corned beef on rye into the lives of many. "What great sandwiches have in common is that they're built with care and made to carry," he explains. But that's not all – a quintessential noshing experience requires a pickle, and you are practically obligated to order one of Alex's genuine homemade dills.

"I make 50-year-old potato salad fresh every day," he says with a wink. For the deli man, life is about the deli.

"Good food and a smile were the recipe to the deli's success," says Alex, whose stint at The Market ended this year. A dedicated soup evangelist, he calls his Cheeseburger Soup a bowl of comfort. It's a recipe that takes the great American cheeseburger and transforms it into a creamy, flavor-packed goulash.

# ALEX'S
# Cheeseburger Soup

*makes 4 servings*

## SOUP

| | |
|---|---|
| 1/2 | pound lean ground beef |
| 1/2 | cup chopped onion |
| 1/2 | cup shredded carrots |
| 1/2 | cup chopped celery stalk |
| 1/2 | teaspoon dried basil |
| 1/2 | teaspoon dried parsley |
| 3 | tablespoons butter, divided |
| 2 | cups chicken broth |
| 2 | cups peeled and diced potatoes |
| 1 | cup of Velveeta processed cheese, cubed |
| 3/4 | cup milk |
| 1/2 | teaspoon salt |
| 1/4 | teaspoon pepper, freshly-cracked |
| | sour cream |
| | diced cooked bacon, for garnish |

**1.** Brown the ground beef in 3-quart saucepan. Drain and set aside. In the same pan add 1 tablespoon butter, onions, carrots, parsley flakes, basil, and celery. Sauté until tender. Add the broth, potatoes and ground beef and bring to a boil. Reduce heat, cover and simmer 10 to 12 minutes or until the potatoes are tender.

**2.** In small skillet, melt remaining butter. Cook and stir for 3 to 5 minutes. Add to the soup and bring to a boil. Cook and stir for 2 minutes. Reduce heat to low. Stir in the cheese, milk, salt and pepper. Cook and stir until cheese melts. Remove from heat.

**3.** To serve, re-warm the soup on low heat. Ladle into 4 warm bowls, top each with a dollop of sour cream and sprinkle with the diced bacon.

# "Pickle Barrel" FRIED DILLS

*makes 6–8 servings*

It was at the Duchess Drive-In located in Atkins, Arkansas, where Bernell "Fatman" Austin first began deep-frying dill pickles. Pickles are to deli cuisine what sauce is to French food, and Alex schleps barrels of his own crunchy dills to the Market, great with sandwiches or for frying and serving as appetizers. Offer the fried dills along with ranch dressing or other creamy sauce for dipping.

## PICKLES

| | |
|---|---|
| 1 | cup all-purpose flour |
| 1/4 | cup cornstarch |
| 1 | teaspoon baking powder |
| 1/4 | teaspoon salt |
| 1 | cup ice water |
| 1 | egg yolk |
| | vegetable oil, for deep-frying |
| 4 | dill pickles, sliced 1/4" thick |

**1.** Stir flour, cornstarch, baking powder and salt into large bowl. Make a well in center; add water, and egg yolk, all at once. Stir with wire whisk to make a smooth batter. Cover bowl and refrigerate 30 minutes.

**2.** Heat at least 2"es of oil in deep fryer or large saucepan to 375° F. In batches, dip pickle slices in the batter to coat evenly and lightly. Fry without crowding in hot oil until golden and crisp, 1 ½ to 2 minutes. Drain on paper towels and serve at once.

# BBQ

## HOLY Smoke

**Stan Riley's enterprise is deeply rooted** in this town. His culinary credentials were hard-earned under the tutelage of Harold Yoho, who introduced Southern Pride woodburning smokers to Ohio and who many consider the father of barbeque in Columbus. "He was a real bootstrap entrepreneur and a great mentor," says Stan, who started out washing dishes for Yoho's catering service during high school.

He worked alongside Harold's son Art throughout college days, and in 2002 the two men became partners. Three years later, each man went his own way with Art focusing on equipment sales and Stan re-branding as Holy Smoke, setting out with a samurai's single-minded approach to barbeque.

"Art and I spent a lot of time talking about the sacredness of what we were doing – cooking whole animals with whole trees, the alchemy of smoke and meat," explains Stan. "We concluded that the craft of barbeque is primordial – it's been around for at least tens of thousands of years."

During hard times in the South, barbecue was the method folks used to add flavor and tenderness to even the most inexpensive cuts of meat, and while it still has a strong connection to that region of the country, Stan insists that barbeque styles are regionally specific, as the choice of wood varies from place to place. "We use shagbark hickory, pignut hickory, and cherrywood in the smokers, harvested from a local tree farm, and we chop it as we need it." He explains that freshly-cut wood provides more flavor as it smolders – the less it has been exposed to the air, the less its loss of potency.

For the juicy Beef Brisket and other hand-held offerings, Auddino's, a local, family-owned bakery, supplies fresh Italian rolls to Holy Smoke. "With a full crunch on the outside yet soft on the inside, they the keep the meat in the bun," says Stan. "It shows we pay attention to the small things."

# Not Like Any Other Slaw, MAN!

*makes 2–4 servings*

Holy Smoke's side dish has a homey, tended-to quality that sets it apart from the typical version served at most barbeque joints. This crisp, rollicking-good combo of farm-fresh vegetables elevates humble shredded cabbage to something truly spectacular.

## VEGETABLE MIX

| | |
|---|---|
| 1 | cup shredded green cabbage |
| 1/2 | cup julienned carrots |
| 1/2 | cup julienned celery root |
| 1/2 | cup julienned snow peas |
| 1/2 | cup julienned fennel |

Combine all cut vegetables in a large mixing bowl. Set aside.

## THE DISH

| | |
|---|---|
| 8 | ounces mayonnaise |
| 2 | tablespoons sugar |
| 2 | ounces apple cider vinegar |
| 1/2 | teaspoon celery seed |
| 1 | tablespoon shaved ginger |
| | salt |
| | black pepper, freshly-cracked |
| | vegetable mix (from left) |

1. In a medium bowl, whisk together the mayonnaise, sugar, apple cider vinegar, celery seed, and shaved ginger. Adjust seasonings to taste. Pour dressing over the vegetables and stir to combine.

2. Transfer to a serving bowl and pass family-style around the table.

This Holy Smoke-inspired dish is a perfect balance of sweet, salty, and meaty, framed by a kiss of smoke, hugged by the robust sauce, and licked by fire. "I recommend chunks over chips on the grill," explains Stan. "A larger size means less deterioration of the wood's character and it won't burn up nearly as fast. Also, since there's no water, there's no steam – which is not the same as smoke – so we avoid it." Choose your favorite Ohio red wine for the gastrique, and serve with plenty of crusty bread for mopping up the flavorful sauce.

# Smoked Pork Chops
## WITH RED WINE GASTRIQUE

*makes 2 servings*

### THE GASTRIQUE

| | |
|---|---|
| 8 | ounces red wine |
| 8 | ounces sugar |
| 1/4 | cup dried currants |

Simmer wine and sugar in small, heavy-bottomed non-reactive saucepan over high heat until syrupy and reduce to ¼ cup, about 15 minutes. Add the dried currants, cover, and remove from heat. Set aside.

### MAIN DISH

| | |
|---|---|
| 2 | (12-ounce) bone-in pork chops, frenched |
| 2 | teaspoons kosher salt |
| 1 | teaspoon black pepper, freshly-cracked |
| 1 | teaspoon onion salt |
| 1 | teaspoon garlic powder |
| | red wine gastrique (from left) |

1. Pre-heat grill (or smoker) to around 350° F. (low to medium setting).

2. Mix together kosher salt, black pepper, onion salt, and garlic powder. Rub spice mixture over the chops and shake off any excess.

3. Throw in dry wood pieces (your favorite flavor is fine) and put them off to the side to create indirect smoke. Let it get going a bit before you put the chops on.

4. Cook the chops over the wood smoke until internal temperature reaches 145° F. Remove from heat, cover, and let rest for about 10 minutes before serving.

5. To serve, add chops to 2 warmed plates. Gently re-heat gastrique and spoon over the top of each, along with a portion of the currants.

# HUBERT'S Polish KITCHEN

**To join his family** already settled in Columbus, Hubert Wilamowski bid farewell to his farm in northwest Poland in 2004, and brought his authentic sausage recipes and butchery skills along with him. He became part of the Market family, working side-by-side with Annemarie Wong at North Market Poultry and Game before taking the leap into his own foodservice venture.

In 2010, joined in the kitchen by his brother Piotrek, Hubert originated Hania's Olde World Cuisine, beginning with a few family recipes. Sticking to their roots, they expanded offerings to include a range of traditional favorites and garnered a faithful following.

Re-named Hubert's Polish Kitchen to better focus on the dishes of his homeland, the Wilamowski enterprise features true Polish cooking, an orphaned culinary craft in this part of the country – outside of ethnic neighborhoods in Cleveland. "Descendants of immigrants remember 'grandmother dishes' from their childhood," explains Hubert, "but what draws other folks to the food is the comfort factor." Think of creamy mashed potatoes, stuffed cabbage rolls, homemade sausages, hearty soups, and on

and on – this is not haute cuisine, but it's the kind of food you can hug like a warm blanket, thrillingly free of high-minded ideals. The only thing missing is polka music.

Using as many local and organic ingredients as possible and relying on recipes from the old country, Hubert's robust, made-from-scratch dishes exceed expectations. "We can barely keep up with the demand for pierogies," explains Hubert. Among the most irresistible dishes, the plump, crescent-shaped dumplings are filled with potato, cream cheese and onions, sauerkraut and mushrooms, and blueberries. They are drenched in butter sauce and topped with sour cream or sautéed onions.

As the Poles say, "Eat, drink, and loosen your belt."

The Polish wedding is legendary as a time when family and friends get together and two families unite. If you've ever attended a Polish wedding, you've probably eaten these pastries, considered essential to the joyous occasion. Traditional *chruściki* (meaning twigs of a tree) are delicate, fried sweet-dough crullers, sprinkled with powdered sugar, and shaped like angel wings. It's impossible to have only one.

# Polish "Angel Wings"

*makes 4 dozen cookies*

## COOKIES

| | |
|---|---|
| 1 | egg |
| 5 | egg yolks |
| 1/4 | cup granulated sugar |
| 1/2 | teaspoon salt |
| 1/4 | cup heavy cream |
| 2 | cups all-purpose flour |
| | vegetable oil, for deep-frying |
| | confectioners' sugar |

1. Using a stand mixer, whisk egg, egg yolks, granulated sugar, salt, and heavy cream until thick and lemon-colored, about 5 minutes.

2. Change to the dough hook and gradually mix in the flour until the dough forms and pulls away from the bowl. Turn out onto a floured board, and knead for 8 to 10 minutes, adding flour if necessary, until the dough is smooth, soft, and elastic.

3. On a floured surface, roll dough very thin. Working with half of the dough at a time, cut into 2"-wide strips. Cut these strips on the diagonal at 4" intervals. To form the wing shape, make a slit in the center of each strip of dough. Then pull one end through the slit to form a bow.

4. Heat the oil in a cast-iron frying pan to 375° F., and fry, a few at a time, for about 1 minute, until lightly browned, turning once with a tong.

5. Immediately remove from the oil, drain on brown paper bags. Dust cookies with confectioners' sugar and repeat, cooking 3 cookies at a time until finished. Store in tightly covered, wax paper-lined tins until ready to serve.

# "BIGOS"
# Polish Hunter's Stew
## with Horseradish Sour Cream

*makes 6-8 servings*

Hubert says he cooks dishes that most people can't even pronounce. His native dish (say "bee-ghos") is a savory Polish stew of cabbage and meat. Its name means "to douse," since Bigos is traditionally doused with wine. The centuries-old dish was originally made with wild game, but over time it has become a stew of many domestic meats. As with others stews, Bigos can be refrigerated and then reheated later – its flavor intensifies when reheated.

### THE HORSERADISH SOUR CREAM

| | |
|---|---|
| I | cup sour cream |
| I | tablespoon prepared horseradish |
| | olive oil |
| | salt |
| | black pepper, freshly-cracked |

Combine sour cream, horseradish and a drizzle of olive oil in a small bowl and mix until thoroughly combined. Season with salt and pepper to taste.

## STEW

| | |
|---|---|
| 4 | slices smoked bacon |
| 1 | pound Polish kielbasa, sliced into 1/2" pieces |
| 1 1/2 | pound cubed pork stew meat |
| 1/4 | cup all-purpose flour |
| 4 | garlic cloves, chopped |
| 1 1/2 | cups onion, diced |
| 2 | medium carrots, diced |
| 2 | cups dried porcini mushrooms, sliced |
| 4 | cups shredded green cabbage |
| 1 | (16 ounce) jar sauerkraut, rinsed and drained |
| 1 | cup dry red wine |
| 2 | bay leaves |
| 2 | teaspoons dried basil |
| 2 | teaspoons dried marjoram |
| 1 1/2 | tablespoons paprika |
| 1/4 | teaspoon salt |
| 1/8 | teaspoon black pepper, freshly-cracked |
| 1/8 | teaspoon caraway seed, crushed |
| 1/8 | teaspoon cayenne pepper |
| 1 | dash Worcestershire sauce |
| 8 | cups beef stock |
| 2 | tablespoons tomato paste |
| 1 1/2 | cups diced tomatoes |
| | horseradish sour cream (from left) |
| | chives, finely chopped, for garnish |

1. Heat a large skillet over medium heat. Add the bacon and kielbasa; cook andstir until the bacon has rendered its fat and sausage is lightly browned. Use a slotted spoon to remove the meat and transfer to a large casserole or Dutch oven.

2. Coat the cubes of pork lightly with flour and fry them in the bacon drippings over medium-high heat until golden brown. Use a slotted spoon to transfer the pork to the casserole. Add the garlic, onion, carrots, mushrooms, cabbage and sauerkraut. Reduce heat to medium; cook and stir until the carrots are soft, about 10 minutes.

3. Deglaze the pan with the red wine. Season with bay leaf, basil, marjoram, paprika, salt, pepper, caraway seeds and cayenne pepper; cook for 1 minute.

4. Mix in Worcestershire sauce, beef stock, tomato paste and tomatoes. Heat through just until boiling. Pour the vegetables and all of the liquid into the casserole dish with the meat. Cover with a lid. Bake in the preheated oven at 350° F. for 2 ½ to 3 hours, until meat is very tender. Remove from the oven and let sit for 15 minutes before serving.

5. To serve, ladle the stew into warmed serving bowls. Add a dollop of the horseradish sour cream on top of each and sprinkle with chopped chives. Serve mashed potatoes and good rye bread alongside.

# jeni's

## SPLENDID ICE creams

**We suspect that she sprinkles fairy dust** on her creations. How else could every one of her ice cream flavors taste so good? Jeni Britton Bauer, the brightest star in the North Market firmament, is celebrated not only for her virtuosity, but also for a brilliant, restless creativity.

Practically everyone in Columbus knows the story about how a young woman worked her way through art school making pastries in a local French bakery, flirted with the idea of becoming a perfumer, then turned her attention to frozen desserts. "My interests all sort of collided with ice cream," says Jeni, who calls her creations "edible perfumes."

"Art is part of my life, part of my DNA," she explains. "Ice cream making is a craft that transports you in the same way art does." In August of 1996, Jeni began making frozen revelations in a little two-gallon batch freezer and selling from a tiny space at the Market she called "Scream." By 2002, having learned the hard lessons of a start-up business, she re-branded as Jeni's Splendid Ice Creams and the rest, quite literally, is ice cream history.

She brings an artist's imagination and wit to the table, matching flavors and textures in the most unexpected ways. Although Jeni draws from many influences, she singles out the North Market community as her earliest inspiration. "The Market is full of sensory experiences," she says. "It's where I learned to combine the bounty of growers and producers, and it's still the driving force in everything we do."

"We try to make the best ice cream we possibly can, different from the way ice cream is typically made and different from the way ingredients are typically sourced," explains Jeni. "When you eat our Vanilla Bean ice cream you're connected with luscious milk and cream from Snowville's cows and high-quality vanilla beans grown on the Ndali Estate in Uganda. We want to slow you down, to tell you the story, so that it becomes a bigger experience than just ice cream."

# The Buckeye State Banana Split

The ice cream sundae, invented in Ithaca, New York in 1892, had already become a staple of American soda fountains when David Strickler began tinkering behind the counter at the Tassell Pharmacy in Latrobe, Pennsylvania. He sliced a banana down the middle, dipped three scoops of different ice cream flavors in between the banana halves, then added dollops of fruit toppings – an achievement he called the "Banana Split Sundae." With rich, salty peanut butter and crunchy bits of dark chocolate, Jeni's splendiferous Buckeye State ice cream becomes the main attraction in this "split" from tradition. (If a hand-held torch in unavailable, caramelize the sugar on the top rack of the broiler, watching carefully to be sure the sugar doesn't burn).

## THE SPLIT

| | |
|---|---|
| 1 | banana, peeled and sliced lengthwise |
| 1 – 2 | teaspoons raw sugar |
| 1 | scoop Jeni's Ndali Estate Vanilla Bean ice cream |
| 1 | scoop Jeni's Buckeye State ice cream |
| 1 | scoop Jeni's Double-Toasted Coconut ice cream |
| 2 | tablespoons chocolate syrup |
| 2 | tablespoons crushed pineapple |
| 2 | tablespoons strawberry topping * |
| | whipped cream |
| 3 | maraschino cherries, finely-chopped, for garnish |

* Wash, remove the stems, and roughly chop 1 pint of fresh strawberries. Combine strawberries, ⅓ cup sugar, and 1 teaspoon vanilla in a saucepan. Cook over medium-high heat, stirring occasionally, until sauce thickens, about 15 minutes. Remove from heat. In a blender, puree about ⅓ of the sauce, then mix back into remaining topping. Store in refrigerator.

1. Place banana halves on a sheet pan, cut side up. Sprinkle each half with enough raw sugar to coat the tops of the bananas. Light a blowtorch and wave in a circular motion over the raw sugar until it bubbles and liquefies into a golden brown, which will harden into a crunchy glassine layer.

2. Place the banana halves sugar side up on an oval plate or shallow bowl. In between the banana halves, add 1 scoop of Buckeye State ice cream at the center and 1 scoop each of Vanilla Bean and Coconut ice creams on either side. Top the Buckeye State ice cream with chocolate syrup, Vanilla Bean ice cream with strawberry topping, and Coconut ice cream with crushed pineapple. Add a generous dollop of whipped cream to the top of each scoop, and sprinkle with the chopped cherries.

# Lan Viet

## MARKET

**The old Quonset hut**-housed North Market reminded Thang Nguyen of the street markets in his native Vietnam. A refugee from the Communist takeover of South Vietnam, he had arrived in Columbus with his family in 1975, hoping for a new life and new beginning. He would eventually become a vendor at the Market, preparing sumptuous native dishes and sharing the culture of his homeland.

Lan Pham, her husband, Thanh Le and son Khanh left Vietnam much later and under very different circumstances. After Thanh earned a Ph.D. degree in London, he accepted a research position at OSU and arrived in Columbus with his family in tow. Khanh began cooking at the Market, and in 2009 he convinced his mother to purchase the business from Thang.

Lan starts her days early each morning, preparing for a menu of Vietnamese street foods from the highest quality ingredients delivered daily. She has an irrepressible spirit and an infectious smile that perfectly complement her enormous passion for sharing the food of her homeland, in particular a fragrant, steaming bowl of rice-noodle soup served with fresh herbs, a cult favorite among marketgoers.

Pho (pronounced fuh), the national dish of Vietnam, is eaten for breakfast and all through the day. The secret of pho is in its long cooking time, extracting all the meaty, marrowy goodness from beef bones and chicken bones. Huge pots are left to boil away all day, so the broth achieves a remarkable depth of flavor – the broth gives pho its life and soul.

Once the footbath-size bowl is put in front of you, you are beckoned to intensify your broth with hoisin or sriracha and squeeze in a few lime wedges. A drop of one, a squeeze of another – to each his or her own. Dig in with a pair of chopsticks in your dominant hand and your soup spoon in the other. This gives you the advantage of picking up noodles with your chopsticks and sipping the broth with your spoon to the very last drop.

A typical Vietnamese dinner consists of jasmine rice and a few dishes, always finishing with a substantial soup. Lan Pham combines catfish and shrimp in her refreshing soup, brightened with tamarind and tomatoes and spiked with chili-based sambal. A big squeeze of lime pulls it all together. While catfish is traditional in Vietnam, you may use tuna, salmon or other fish, and cooked white rice may substitute for vermicelli.

# Fragrant Fish Soup
## WITH TAMARIND AND SAMBAL

*makes 6 servings*

### SOUP

| | |
|---|---|
| 1 | package dry rice noodle (vermicelli) |
| 2 | pounds catfish nuggets |
| 1 | pound peeled large shrimp |
| | salt |
| | black pepper, freshly-cracked |
| 2 | (32-ounce) cans low-sodium chicken broth |
| 1 | tablespoon tamarind powder |
| 1 | tablespoon sambal |
| 1/4 | cup of fish sauce (nuoc mam) |
| 2 | medium-sized tomatoes, sliced into small wedges |
| 1 | cup of minced green onion |
| 1 | cup of minced dill |
| 1/2 | cup of minced cilantro |
| | lime wedges |
| | jalapeño pepper slices |

1. Cook vermicelli according to the package directions, rinse with cold water and drain.

2. Lightly season the catfish and shrimp with salt and pepper. Combine chicken broth, tamarind powder, sambal, and fish sauce in a large pot. Bring the mixture to a boil. Add the catfish nuggets to the soup. Bring back to a boil, then lower heat and simmer for 5 minutes. Add the tomatoes and simmer for an additional 3 minutes. Add the shrimp and simmer for another 2 minutes. Add extra salt and tamarind powder to taste.

3. To serve, portion the rice noodles into 6 large bowls. Divide the green onion among the bowls. Pour the broth over the noodles, enough to completely cover. Top each serving with dill and cilantro. Pass wedges of lime and slices of jalapeño around the table.

These light and healthy summer rolls are filled with cooked shrimp, rice noodles, and plenty of fresh herbs and vegetables for flavor and crunch. Once your ingredients are prepped, the rolling fun begins as sheets of rice paper are softened in water and used for the wrappers. Dipped in spicy peanut sauce, these toothsome rolls are a great hot-weather appetizer or light lunch. "Think of a taco night, only Vietnamese-style," says Khanh. (Shredded roasted beef, pork, or chicken may be substituted for the shrimp).

# "Goi Cuon" Summer Rolls
## with Peanut Dipping Sauce

*makes 18–20 rolls*

### THE ROLLS

| | |
|---|---|
| 20 | rice wrappers (8") |
| I | pound cook shrimp (30 to 40 count) |
| I | package dry rice noodles (vermicelli) |
| 2 | heads of romaine hearts or lettuce |
| I | large cucumber |
| 2 | cups chopped cilantro |
| 1/2 | cup chopped roasted peanuts |

### DIPPING SAUCE

| | |
|---|---|
| I | tablespoon creamy peanut butter |
| 1/2 | teaspoon vegetable oil |
| 2 | cups hoisin sauce |

Melt peanut butter and vegetable oil in a double boiler, stirring to mix well. Add hoisin sauce and continue stirring to combine. Transfer sauce to a bowl and let cool.

1. Cook vermicelli according to the package directions, rinse with cold water and drain. Slice shrimp in half from head to tail (if using beef, pork or chicken, roast and shred into thin slices). Cut romaine heart or lettuce into 4" sections. Slice cucumber into 4" thin strips.

2. Dip each rice wrapper into a bowl of warm water and lay flat on a plate. Place 4 pieces of shrimp on the wrapper, then add two pieces of lettuce, 2 pieces of cucumber, some vermicelli, cilantro and chopped roasted peanuts. Holding firmly in place, fold the sides of the wrapper in envelope-style and form into a roll. Turn the roll so that the seam faces down and the row of shrimp faces up. Repeat with the remaining wrappers and fillings.

3. To serve, arrange rolls around a large platter with the bowl of dipping sauce at the center. (If not serving immediately, keep the rolls tightly covered with plastic wrap at room temperature for up to 2 hours).

# MARKET

**There's a Chinese proverb that goes** something like this: "When you have only two pennies left in the world, buy a loaf of bread with one, and a lily with the other." A flower shop among the culinary offerings at the North Market has been a longstanding tradition.

Martha "Marty" McGreevy has loved flowers for as long as she can remember, and while working for an event planning service, she dreamed of someday running her own shop. "When the flower peddler at the Market offered to sell the business," she explains, "I decided this was my moment."

Market Blooms debuted as a bucket shop. Marty gathered flowers, set them in buckets in front of her space and sold them by the bunch. "Folks come here to eat or buy groceries, and our flowers provide a feel-good moment," she says, "but I wanted to do more." She became, in her words, a "guerilla-trained" designer, offering a selection of hand-tied bouquets and custom arrangements. Then in 1995, Bob Mangia, a local florist with an innovative flair for design, joined the staff, and according to Marty, "I knew the stars had aligned to realize my vision." You can design your own arrangement, or you are welcome to bring in your own container and they will create an arrangement just for you. "When designing yourself, the rule is just to keep it simple," says Marty, who also offers advice on making your bouquet last longer. "Fresh water is the lifeblood of cut flowers," she insists. "Change the water every day and re-trim the ends of the stems every two days."

The location of Marty's shop in the center spot of the hall is no accident. Administration wanted to encourage the relationship between people who love fresh food and fresh, colorful flowers. "The Market is a joyful place," says Marty, "and I think we provide the exclamation point."

# BLO

# FLOWERS for Home Entertaining

The harmonious relationship between food and flowers is best explained in the Dutch saying, "Food feeds the body, but flowers feed the soul." Like many artists, Marty often finds inspiration in her surroundings, and as the Market's florist, she is the resident expert on arrangements for the dinner table. "Flowers are an essential part of any gathering regardless of size," says Marty, "and as much a part of the dining experience as the menu and the place settings." She offers her advice for home entertaining.

Varieties and styles will vary depending on the environment and mood you are trying to achieve. Choose what you like, flowers that compliment your home and shed light on your spirit and personality.

For a table top arrangement, use flowers with little or no scent. Consider the fragrance of the flowers and decide if it will interfere or enhance the meal. You do not want guests to be overpowered by the floral arrangements.

Don't try for anything too elaborate. If you have multiple arrangements, make sure to leave room for dishes, especially if you are serving family-style. Several small arrangements as opposed to one large one provides a gift for each of your guests to take home and enjoy.

When designing, just make sure all flower heads are visible. Each bloom wants to enjoy the dinner party! Insert the showiest of the large, featured flowers into the center.

Think outside the vase (box) when selecting a container. Anything that holds water can be utilized – jars, pitchers, bowls, even hollowed-out green peppers. A table top arrangement should be held in a low container, such as a bowl or compote, so that it does not block diners' views of one another across the table and conversations can flow freely.

Market-inspired arrangements may include fruits and vegetables with flowers. Choose garden veggies and fruits with interesting shapes and colors, such as squash, carrots and beans.

Secure enough greenery to fill in between and around the flowers. Shop your yard (or your neighbors). Grasses, evergreens, or ivy can be trimmed and incorporated into the design. Inserting the stems so that the greens are slightly lower than the level of the flowers, accenting rather than covering them up.

If you're on a budget, use what you have first to free up more money for the showy parts.

# NIDA'S Sushi

**Nida Sujirapinyokul was born and raised in Bangkok,** Thailand, a city that has long attracted migrants from across Asia, so its cuisine, both at vendor carts and in restaurants, blends styles of cooking and influences from many traditions. Her family owned a local coconut refinery, and Nida recalls, "We went out every weekend to the best eating spots in the city."

At age eighteen, she arrived in the U.S. to study finance at Xavier University in Cincinnati, juggling a full class load while working at a local Thai restaurant. After four years and armed with her degree, she returned home to accept a job in advertising, and where she met her American husband, Christopher Perry, a geologist with the Ohio Department of Natural Resources.

Food stalls are scattered throughout Bangkok, and some are clustered together in markets offering fresh fish, meats, fruit, vegetables, and cooked foods. So when Nida moved to Columbus and Chris introduced her to the North Market, her passion for the cuisine of her homeland had found the perfect outlet. To hone her skills, she studied at the California Sushi Academy under the critical eyes of Japanese masters. After graduation, she apprenticed with a local sushi chef, and after a few months she was ready to go into business for herself. Since 2001, she has been part of the North Market's tight-knit community.

One of the pleasures of Nida's Sushi is the display of artistry in the open kitchen counter – the deft, sure strokes of the razor-sharp and brilliantly gleaming knives that turn humble ingredients into works of art – gleaming sashimi, picturesque sushi and inspired California rolls, directly from the chef's hands to you. And what is considered proper etiquette for eating raw fish arranged atop sushi rice? "It depends," says Nida. "Sometimes I use chopsticks, and sometimes I just use my fingers."

# "Tom Yum" BLOODY MARY

*makes 1 serving*

It's a Bloody Mary with a Thai accent, created by Nida at her Short North restaurant, Thai on High. The traditional pick-me-up is revitalized with the spicy ingredients of Thai cuisine's "tom yum" broth. Fragrant kaffir leaves can be floated on the drink or you can chop a few leaves to mix with the drink and strengthen the exotic flavors. Go ahead, Thai one on.

### THE TOM YUM MIX

| | |
|---|---|
| 2 | teaspoons finely-chopped lemon grass |
| 1/2 | teaspoon salt |
| 1/2 | teaspoon black pepper, freshly-cracked |
| 3 | teaspoons sugar |
| 1 | tablespoon of chili garlic paste |
| 1 | large jar tomato juice (32 ounces) |
| | juice of 2 limes |
| 2 | tablespoons galangal paste |

Combine ingredients in a nonreactive container. Refrigerate until thoroughly chilled, at least 2 hours and up to overnight.

### THE DRINK

| | |
|---|---|
| 6 | ounces tom yum mix (from left) |
| 2 | ounces vodka |
| | kaffir lime leaves, for garnish |

Combine tom yum mix and vodka in a mixing glass filled with ice. Shake vigorously and strain into a tall glass filled with fresh ice. Garnish with kaffir leaves.

The ideal Pad Thai has an equilibrium between the forces of sweet, salty, and sour components. Fish sauce, or "Nam Pla" in Thai, although more pungent, functions very much like Chinese soy sauce, and nearly everyone without the allergy loves the ground peanuts. Nida's Pad Thai is relatively light and dry, a version closest to the "street food" of Thailand. Soft tofu is gently embedded, although you may take creative liberties and substitute beef, chicken, or shrimp. To properly prepare, she suggests getting individual ingredients ready in small bowls.

# PAD THAI, North Market-Style

*makes 4 servings*

## MAIN DISH

| | |
|---|---|
| 8 | ounces dried wide, flat rice noodles |
| 1/4 | cup fresh lime juice, plus lime wedges for serving (3 limes) |
| 3 | tablespoons fish sauce |
| 1/3 | cup tamarind juice |
| 1 | teaspoon chili sauce, such as Sriracha |
| 1 | tablespoon packed dark-brown sugar |
| 2 | tablespoons peanut oil |
| 2 | large eggs, lightly whisked |
| 1 | package (14 ounces) extra firm tofu, drained, sliced into 1/8" rectangles |
| 1 | cup carrots, peeled and shredded |
| 3 | garlic cloves, minced |
| 8 | scallions, white and green parts separated and thinly sliced |
| | sea salt |
| 3 | tablespoons roasted salted peanuts, crushed in a mortar and pestle or food processor |
| 1/4 | cup fresh cilantro leaves |
| 2 | limes, quartered |

1. Bring enough water to a boil to cover the noodles. Turn off heat and immerse rice noodles in hot water for 3 to 5 minutes until cooked through but still firm. Rinse with cold water for 30 seconds and drain well.

2. In a small bowl, whisk together lime juice, tamarind juice, fish sauce, chili sauce, and brown sugar.

3. In a large nonstick skillet, heat ½ teaspoon oil over medium-high heat. Add eggs, swirl to coat bottom, and cook until just set, about 1 minute. Transfer eggs to a cutting board, loosely roll up, and cut crosswise into thin strips. Add 4 teaspoons oil to skillet and heat. Add tofu in a single layer and cook until golden brown on both sides. Transfer to cutting board.

4. Add 1 ½ teaspoons oil, carrots, garlic, and scallion whites to skillet and cook until softened, about 5 minutes. Add lime juice mixture and bring to a simmer. Add noodles and cook, stirring frequently, about 1 minute, until the mixture is evenly distributed. Add eggs and tofu and gently toss to combine. Season with salt to taste.

5. Transfer to a warmed bowl, scatter the peanuts over the top, garnish with cilantro leaves, and serve family-style around the table, passing a dish of lime sections alongside.

**The shop's personality** really lies in the innovative kitchen accessories it offers for any level of enthusiast to enjoy. "I sell things I like myself, and I've built up a customer base that likes what I like," says Kay Davenport, whose enterprise celebrates the love of cooking and entertaining.

After traveling in Europe where, in her words, "my notions of food were expanded," she became a purposeful retailer, intent on stocking kitchenware that holds up to her high standards. "Everything in the store has to make sense," explains Kay. "At the Market, I don't have extra space for frivolous or marginal-quality items – everything has to have a solid function as well as quality that will hold up."

Kay and her team love matching customers to just the right set of tools that will enhance their culinary pursuits, especially when so many are beginning to mimic restaurant-style food in their own homes. "What restaurant chefs have that home cooks want are really good pots and pans," says Kay Davenport, "pans that respond to temperatures and distribute heat evenly." The shop has many specialty items, but Kay is especially fond of the Beka enameled aluminum for cooking with high heat. "The manufacturer puts in the extra effort and expense to get the bonding correct," she explains. "The result is a pan that will last."

Over the years, stock has expanded, and you can now expect to be surprised. "Who would have ever thought we would end up selling hardware," asks Kay, "but the carpenter's microplane has now become a staple of the kitchen for grating hard cheese, whole nutmeg, ginger, and chocolate or zesting lemons."

"Marketgoers really count on us to know the merchandise," says Kay. Whether it's about preparation, presentation, or the tools you need to prepare a special dish, North Market Cookware turns mere cooking into artistic pursuit.

# NORTH MARKET COOKWARE

Fresh ginger adds a warm and comforting aroma to an especially good winter risotto. The microplane does an amazing job of grating even the most fibrous knob of ginger into a juicy, paste-like consistency. The tiny, ultrasharp teeth also make quick work of grating carrots and hard cheese for this flavorful dish. Properly cooked, the risotto should be soft and creamy, retaining an *al dente* bite and separate grains. It must be eaten at once as it continues to cook in its own heat.

# A Warming Winter Risotto

*makes 2 servings*

**MAIN DISH**

| | |
|---|---|
| 3 1/2 | cups low-sodium chicken broth |
| 2 | tablespoons olive oil |
| 1/2 | medium white onion, finely-diced |
| 1 | tablespoon freshly-grated ginger |
| 1 | small carrot, peeled and freshly-grated |
| 3 | cloves garlic, peeled and chopped |
| 1 | cup arborio rice |
| 1/4 | cup white wine |
| 2 | tablespoons freshly-grated parmesan cheese |

1. Heat the oil in a large, heavy-bottomed saucepan over medium heat. Add the onions and sauté until slightly translucent, about 2 minutes. Add the ginger, carrots, and garlic, and sauté for another 1 to 2 minutes.

2. Add the rice and stir with a wooden spoon so that the grains are coated with the oil. Stir in the wine and simmer until the liquid is fully absorbed.

3. Begin adding broth, one ladleful at a time, stirring constantly until the liquid is absorbed. Continue adding ladles of hot stock and stirring the rice while the liquid is absorbed. As it cooks, the rice will take on a creamy consistency as it begins to release its natural starches. Remove from the heat.

4. To serve, divide the risotto between 2 warmed bowls and spoon 1 tablespoon of the grated cheese over the top of each. Serve immediately.

# NORTH MARKET
## Poultry and Game

**Sometimes you simply have to follow your instincts, for goodness sake. When the young woman from Toledo contemplated an enterprise at the Market, it seemed like a sensible notion, in her words, "to get back-to-basics." Since 1995, Annemarie Wong and her staff at North Market Poultry and Game have been on a mission to re-connect the Columbus community with "real food."**

As Market folks bid farewell to digs in the old Quonset hut, the original poultry vendor decided to drop out. It gave Annemarie an opportunity to fill the slot, intending to offer as many locally-raised products as possible, sourcing them directly from local family farms. "It's a very traditional way of doing business," she says, "and I prefer it the old way."

"We opened for business just before Thanksgiving," she recalls, "and we sold over 200 free-range turkeys from a sustainable farm in New Carlisle. Before long, we had other small-scale farmers coming to us with fresh, locally-raised venison, bison, chickens, geese, pheasants, ducks, and rabbits." As the business matured and the

range of products expanded, her personal connection deepened, and Annemarie began regular visits to the farms she represents. "I take my role as intermediary between farmer and customer very seriously," she explains. "If I am to be a trusted source, I want to see things for myself."

On one of her favorite excursions, Annemarie drives up to Cardington to meet with Brooke Hayes at Speckled Hen Farm, supplier of "Cornish-Rock" chickens, pasture-raised without growth hormones or antibiotics. These slow-growing birds take twice as long to mature as conventional industry birds, and the meat is firm and flavorful. "It tastes the way chicken used to taste," insists Annemarie.

It's most often associated with a certain holiday in November, but according to Chef Seifert of Spagio, a crispy, juicy turkey can be enjoyed at any special occasion dinner. "Start with a good bird," advises the chef. He is passionate in his belief in dining as a communal event. "I think cooking should bring people together," he says. "We should shop together, chop vegetables together, and cook together – then we eat together."

# CHEF HUBERT SEIFERT'S
# Roast Turkey with Bread Pudding

*makes 6 servings*

### THE BREAD PUDDING

| | |
|---|---|
| 2 | tablespoons butter |
| 3 | eggs, beaten |
| 3 | cups milk |
| 1/4 | cup cooked bacon crumbles |
| 1 | tablespoon chopped roasted garlic |
| 2 | tablespoons chopped parsley |
| 2 | tablespoons chopped green onion |
| | salt |
| | black pepper, freshly-cracked |
| 6 | cups white bread, cut into 1/2" cubes |

Butter six 4-ounce ramekins. In a large bowl, whisk the eggs and milk. Add the bacon, garlic, parsley and green onion and season with salt and pepper. Add the bread cubes and let sit until the liquid is absorbed. Spoon the bread mixture into the ramekins. Place them in a large roasting pan and fill the pan with water half way up the ramekin sides. Bake for 45 minutes at 350° F. Raise the temperature to 400° F. and bake 10 more minutes.

### THE TURKEY

| | |
|---|---|
| 1 | (12 to 15 pound) turkey, halved and de-boned, keeping leg bones attached |
| 2 | sticks butter, softened |
| 3 | tablespoons lemon juice |
| 2 | tablespoons fresh thyme, chopped |
| | Kosher salt |
| | black pepper, freshly-cracked |
| 3 | garlic cloves, chopped |

1. Preheat oven to 350° F. In a bowl, combine butter, lemon juice, thyme, salt and white pepper. Refrigerate for at least 15 minutes. Season the turkey with salt and pepper. Gently rub the butter mixture and the garlic under the skin. Place turkey halves in a roasting pan, and roast for one hour (or to an internal temperature of 160° F).

2. Remove the turkey from the oven and let it rest for 15 to 20 minutes. If making gravy, reserve the juices in the roasting pan.

3. Carve the turkey and serve bread pudding alongside.

For those who prefer to try before you buy, Annemarie operates an adjoining stand called Kitchen Little where an ever-changing menu of dishes demonstrates the quality of the meats – and paper-hat-clad line cooks inspire a feeling of bonhomie. Free-roaming chickens provide much firmer and flavorful meat for chicken burgers, a Market favorite.

# "Yard Bird" Burgers
# with Avocado Mayonnaise

*makes 6 servings*

## THE BURGERS

| | |
|---|---|
| 1 1/2 | pounds ground chicken |
| 1/2 | cup chipotle in adobo sauce, ground |
| 1/2 | teaspoon salt |
| 1 | tablespoon brown sugar |
| 1 | egg, beaten |
| 3 | tablespoons chopped cilantro |
| 1/2 | cup panko bread crumbs |
| | olive oil, as needed |
| 6 | sandwich rolls or burger buns, toasted |
| | avocado mayonnaise (from below) |
| | romaine or other greens, for topping |

1. In a large bowl, add the ground chicken, adobo sauce, salt, brown sugar, egg, and bread crumbs and pepper.

2. Divide chicken mix into 6 portions size and using clean hands, gently combine the ingredients and form the chicken mixture into 6 patties.

3. Heat olive oil in a large non-stick skillet over medium heat and fry patties until golden and cooked through, about 5 to 7 minutes per side. Transfer to paper towels and let rest for a few minutes.

4. To assemble, spread a dollop of the mayonnaise mixture on the tops and bottoms of the toasted buns. Place the chicken burgers on the bottom halves of the buns. Top each with romaine and close with the top half of the bun.

## THE MAYONNAISE

| | |
|---|---|
| 1/2 | cup mayonnaise |
| 1 | avocado, pitted, flesh scooped from the skin |
| 1 | teaspoon lime juice, freshly-squeezed |
| 2 – 3 | dashes Tabasco |

Purée all ingredients in blender, scraping down sides occasionally. Set aside.

# Braised Chicken
## with Tuscan Aromas

*makes 4 servings*

It is said that taste is in equal measure scent and flavor, a fact that is never more evident than in the cuisine of Tuscany, according to Chef Kent Rigsby of Rigsby's Kitchen. "This is a soulful recipe from a lunch I had in Tuscany," he recalls, "prepared by Dania Masotti at Ristorante La Chiusa, nestled in the hills halfway between Pienza and Montepulciano. For me, this dish re-captures the scents and aromas of the Tuscan countryside." As they say in Tuscany, *chi mangia senza bere mura a secco*, so enjoy with a bottle of local wine.

### THE TOM YUM MIX

| | |
|---|---|
| 2 | local Cornish Rock chickens |
| 1/4 | cup extra virgin olive oil + extra for drizzle |
| 2 | large yellow onions, coarsely-chopped |
| 5 | carrots, diced |
| 4 | ribs celery, diced |
| | salt |
| | black pepper, freshly-cracked |
| 1 | cup dry white wine |
| 1 | cup chicken stock |
| 2 | tomatoes, coarsely chopped, or 5 canned roma tomatoes, chopped |
| 2 | branches rosemary, leaves only, minced |
| 6 | sprigs fresh thyme, leaves only, chopped |
| 4 | leaves fresh sage, minced |
| 10 | leaves fresh basil, chopped |
| 3 | sprigs Italian parsley, chopped, for garnish |

1. Carve the chickens so you have four boneless breasts and four boneless thighs. Cut each piece in half. Heat the olive oil in a Dutch oven or large sauté pan over high heat until smoking. Sear the chicken pieces until browned on all sides. Remove chicken from the pot and set aside.

2. Add the onion, carrot and celery, season with salt and pepper to taste and cook until the vegetables are soft. Add the white wine, and chicken stock, stirring to dislodge any browned bits from the bottom of the pot. Add the chopped tomatoes and bring to a boil.

3. Return the chicken to the pot, season with salt and pepper, bring back to boil, then lower to a simmer. Cook for about 30 minutes, then add all the herbs. Continue to cook, stirring occasionally for another 45 minutes. (Add a little water to the braise if it seems dry). Taste and adjust seasoning.

4. To serve, arrange the chicken on a large platter. Pour the sauce over the chicken, drizzle with olive oil and sprinkle with chopped parsley.

# NORTH MARKET **SPICES**

**For this modern-day spice merchant,** the road to a world of exotic flavors and aromas began in his youth. Ben Walters remembers feeling inspired by the foods he discovered while traveling in France and Spain. "I was already interested in cooking, and I think it spurred an interest in experimenting with the spices and cooking of different cuisines."

His curious palate nearly landed him in culinary school. Instead, he earned a degree in tourism and took a job with the Columbus Convention & Visitors Bureau. He would eventually succumb to the lure of the Market, and – lucky for us – his idea for a spice shop coincided with a vacancy in the hall. North Market Spices became a reality in 2010.

While herbs and spices are readily available at grocery stores and ethnic food stores in and around the city, there wasn't one place with multiple, fresh varieties. "When you have all the spices in one place, freshness makes a difference, freshly ground versus the stuff you typically find already ground," says Ben. "You can see it and smell it and taste it – we even have tasting spoons."

Ben grinds components to specific coarse sizes and hand-blends select spices and herbs in small batches for quality and consistency, and he creates custom blends for local restaurants and food trucks. He's a culinary superhero dedicated to saving the planet from bland, flavorless food with a veritable smorgasbord of herbs and spices. His shop at the Market has been called the highest concentration of flavor in all of Columbus.

He delights in showing purists, novices and everyone in between how much of a difference good, fresh spices can make in initial food preparation, as the add-on during the cooking process, or as a finishing touch. "Let us embellish your culinary whims," offers Ben. "We'll take any dish from bland to grand."

Popularized by Italian immigrants in Endicott, New York in the 1930s, grilled meat was traditionally served on a skewer with a slice of fresh bread on the side, and prepared most often with small pieces of lamb. But as the city's meaty legacy evolves into a regional food truck favorite, it's now something closer to a proper sandwich, loaded with pieces of marinated and grilled chicken already pulled off the stick. The humble "spiedi" (from the Italian *spiedo* referring to cubes of meat cooked on a skewer) is elevated from ordinary to extraordinary with "Truck Dust" from North Market Spices, an eclectic mix that includes smoked sea salt, twilight pepper, coriander, cumin, guajillo chili, thyme, and brown sugar.

# Chicken Spiedies with "TRUCK DUST"

*makes 4 servings*

## MAIN DISH

| | |
|---|---|
| 3 | boneless chicken breasts |
| 1/3 | cup olive oil |
| 1/4 | cup lemon juice |
| 1/4 | cup white vinegar |
| 2 | garlic cloves, finely-chopped |
| 1 | tablespoon dried parsley |
| 2 | tablespoons "Truck Dust" spice mix |
| 1/2 | teaspoon salt |
| 4 | fresh bread rolls |

1. Dice chicken breasts into 1" cubes. Whisk the olive oil, lemon juice, vinegar, garlic, parsley, spice mix, and salt in a bowl and pour into a re-sealable plastic bag. Add chicken cubes, coat with the marinade, squeeze out excess air, and seal the bag. Marinate in the refrigerator overnight.

2. Preheat grill for medium heat and lightly oil the grate.

3. Remove chicken from marinade and discard used marinade. Thread 5 or 6 chicken cubes onto metal or soaked bamboo skewers and cook on the grill until no longer pink in the center and meat is firm, about 6 to 7 minutes per side.

4. Toast rolls and spread each with some of the reserved marinade. Place a skewer on each roll and carefully remove the skewer, leaving the chicken in the bun.

In this simple and elegant technique, planked salmon steams gently in the heat of the grill, staying incredibly tender and moist. It also picks up lush, smoky aroma from the grill and woodsy flavors from the cedar, along with a burst of fruit wood from the salt. Find cedar shakes at grocery stores with well-stocked grill sections or your local hardware store.

# Salmon Grilled on Cedar Shakes
## WITH APPLEWOOD-SMOKED SALT

*makes 4 servings*

**MAIN DISH**

| | |
|---|---|
| 4 | untreated cedar shakes (planks), soaked in water overnight |
| 4 | (8-ounce) wild salmon fillets, skin on |
| 4 | teaspoons olive oil |
| | applewood-smoked salt |
| 4 | sprigs rosemary |
| | fresh parsley leaves, chopped, for garnish |

1. Prepare an outdoor grill, adjusting temperature for medium-high heat. Place planks on the grill. Cover grill and heat planks 2 to 3 minutes, until dry.

2. Rub salmon fillets with olive oil. Season with smoked salt to taste. Top each portion with a sprig of rosemary.

3. Arrange a fillet skin side down on each plank and place grates on the grill grates. Cook the salmon, covered, until the fish flakes when tested with a fork, about 10 to 12 minutes. (The planks should be approximately 8 inches from the heat; if they catch fire, spray with a little water). Remove the planks from the grill using a long-handled spatula, discard the rosemary sprigs, and gently separate the skin from the salmon.

4. To serve, place a salmon fillet on each of 4 warmed dinner plates and garnish with the chopped parsley.

It's a cocktail as salad, or vice versa. Cris Dehlavi, the consulting mixologist at Middle West Spirits, creates a savory, farm-to-bar refreshment, taking advantage of fresh tomato's natural balance of sweetness and acidity. She pairs a local heirloom with locally-distilled vodka, bright, tangy lemon juice, and the kick of sriracha. With each sip, the drink mingles with lavender salt on the rim of the glass, heightening flavors of the vegetables and adding dimension to the culinary cocktail.

# MAYDAY

*makes 1 drink*

### COCKTAIL

| | |
|---|---|
| 2 | ounces **OYO** Vodka |
| 1/4 | ounce lemon juice, freshly-squeezed |
| 1/3 | cup muddled heirloom tomato |
| 1/4 | cup muddled red bell pepper |
| 2–3 | drops sriracha sauce or Tabasco |
| | pinch of salt |
| | pinch of black pepper, freshly-cracked |
| | lavender salt |
| | fresh basil leaf, for garnish |

Combine vodka, lemon juice, tomato, pepper, bitters, salt and pepper with ice in a cocktail shaker and shake vigorously.

Rim a rocks glass by moistening the edge with a lemon wedge, then dipping the glass into a small plate of the lavender salt.

Strain the drink into the salt-rimmed glass over fresh ice. Garnish with the basil leaf and serve.

# omega ARTISAN BAKING

**She's a Columbus native** who remembers coming to the North Market when it was still housed in the Quonset hut. "When I was a kid, my mother brought me here," recalls Amy Lozier, "and it's the first public place I ever took my own daughter."

After graduating from OSU, Amy worked for book publisher W.W. Norton, allowing her a month off every year and the chance to spend that time with her sister who lived in Switzerland. It was where she fell in love – with bread. After prodding the bakers of Zurich for secrets of their craft, she came home and delved into Bernard Clayton's *The Breads of France*, a book that became her bible. According to Amy, "I still know parts of it by heart."

"I would learn to make each bread," she explains, "and I would make it – oh gosh – two or three times a week until I got it right. If I had extra time, I would make it four or five times!" Obviously, it was time to change gears. She was thrilled with the opportunity to expand her repertoire in the pastry kitchens of a few local restaurants, including Elevator Brewery, where she claims, "I became something of an expert on desserts made with beer."

Later, she jumped at the offer to make soups and salads for Robin Sanfilippo, the North Market's produce vendor. After the Market's baker dropped out, it was Amy's turn. At 52-years-young, she set out to return the art of bread making to its roots at Omega, beginning with good, honest Rustic French, Italian, Sourdough, and Ciabatta, plus a few desserts.

"We've grown dramatically since those days," she explains, "but we still bake in small batches so we can always be in control – that's particularly important with bread. Human hands are involved in every stage, and only the best natural ingredients are used, without chemicals and additives. All these factors contribute to making the very best products."

In early Spring, look for the long, narrow radishes (with red tops that fade to white tips) on display at the Market. Harvesting just after a frost brings out the sweetness in these little beauties. Leave it to the French to perfect the art of the simple pleasure. They enjoy open-faced sandwiches of rustic bread with herbed butter, topped with slices of *les radis petit dejeuner* and a sprinkles of fleur de sel. One of Amy's signature breads (with a local cult following), Rustic French is airy on the inside with a dark crust that gives it a flavor all its own. There is something very satisfying about eating with one's hands, and good bread is the secret to this dexterous treat.

# "French Breakfast" Radish Tartine
## ON RUSTIC FRENCH BREAD
*makes 2 servings*

### THE TARTINE

| | |
|---|---|
| 1 | bunch French Breakfast radishes, greens and bottoms removed |
| 3 | tablespoons unsalted butter, at room temp |
| 1/2 | cup microgreens, finely chopped + extra for garnish |
| 2 | tablespoons fresh chives, finely chopped |
| 2 | slices Omega "Rustic French" bread fleur de sel or other sea salt |

1. Finely chop ⅔ of the radishes, and slice ⅓ of the radishes into thin rounds. Combine butter, microgreens, chives, and the chopped radishes.

2. Spread mixture on bread slices. Shingle sliced radishes over the mixture, overlapping them to evenly cover the bread.

3. Season with salt to taste, and scatter with a few microgreens before serving.

"Strata is the bread pudding of savory egg dishes," says Amy. "Put in whatever you have on hand, or whatever is fresh and seasonal at the Market." A few suggestions: roasted vegetables (onions, mushrooms, carrots, bell peppers) with roasted garlic added to the egg mixture; cooked bacon or sausage with maple syrup and cheddar cheese; rye bread with Swiss cheese, a little mustard and corned beef or pastrami; leftover cooked chicken with any cheese, broccoli, or any other cooked vegetables. Use any cheese you like. Try fresh goat cheese or feta, or a few crumbles of a blue cheese mixed in with something more mild. "This is a great recipe for children," says Amy. "A little help chopping and slicing the bread, and they can make a meal!"

# "STRATA"
# Breakfast Casserole

*makes 4 servings*

## MAIN DISH

| | |
|---|---|
| I | loaf of bread (or a combination of different breads to equal 3/4 to I pound) |
| 6 | eggs |
| 3 | cups milk |
| I | cup cream |
| 3/4 | cup cheese, grated or crumbled |
| | filling ingredients |

1. Use a 9" x 13" pan at least 2 inches deep, either buttered liberally, or if you want to be sure to be able to remove the strada from the pan, you can make a sling of parchment along the length of the pan, greasing the pan and the parchment lightly.

2. Remove crusts from bread (or leave them on if the crusts are soft like Challah) and cut into cubes or slice in ½" slices.

3. In a bowl, combine eggs, milk and cream. Add any flavoring you like to this mixture, such as a cup of sugar for a sweet pudding, a little dried or prepared mustard to go with vegetables, or a couple tablespoons of honey or maple syrup for a sweet/savory mix.

4. Layer half of the bread slices or cubes and top with whatever ingredients you are using. Top with the remainder of the bread. (You don't want to fill the pan too full; remember, you have over four cups of liquid to go into the same pan).

5. Pour the egg mixture over the bread and top with whatever cheese you are using in the pudding. At this point, the pan can be covered and placed in the refrigerator overnight.

6. Remove from the fridge an hour or so before you plan to bake it and let it come to room temperature. This will result in more saturated bread, and a softer consistency.

7. When you are ready to bake, cover pan with aluminum foil and bake at 300° F. for 40 to 45 minutes. (Depending on the ingredients, it may take longer). When the casserole is no longer obviously fluid (when the eggs have cooked and the custard is solid), remove the foil and bake for an additional 10 minutes or so until the top brown.

8. Let cool for 5 minutes before serving. Serve by the spoonful, using a large serving spoon.

# PAM'S
## MARKET popcorn

**It's entirely in keeping with the infectious spirit** of the Market. Pam Tylka's shop is wide open to charges of being gimmicky, but if you give in to nostalgic cravings, you'll enjoy munching on the freshest, best-tasting popcorn you've ever had.

Pam grew up in Chicago, where she remembers her grandpa Ralph, an editor at the *Sun-Times*, popping corn in the family kitchen, and where she and her friends would often wait in line at Garrett's, the Windy City's legendary popcorn shop. After a foodservice career, including a stint at Saban's Place in nearby McCook, she moved to Columbus and, armed with Chicago-built popcorn-making equipment, introduced freshly-popped treats to the Market in 2005.

Good popcorn starts with good kernels. Pam relies on sturdy, high-starch varieties of popping corn grown on farms in Ohio and Indiana. For "naked" popcorn she prefers kernels that produce smaller puffs but have more distinctive flavor, texture, and crunch, "so good," she insists, "they could be enjoyed without butter or salt." For her flavor-coated offerings, however, she uses tender, ball-shaped "mushroom" popcorn with lots of divots and crannies and fluffy "butterfly" popcorn with "wings" protruding from each kernel. All production is done by hand, and each batch is cooked with pure coconut oil in small batches.

Another nod to her Chicago roots comes in the form of cheddar and caramel, a balanced combination of sweet and savory popcorn invented in her hometown. "Some say it is the contrast of salt and sweet that makes this mix irresistable," says Pam. "I think of cheese popcorn and caramel popcorn as yin and yang, complementary opposites – and opposites attract!"

In the old days, theater owners would pump in the fragrant aroma of popcorn to attract moviegoers who were, of course, powerless to resist. Follow your nose to Pam's at the North Market and surrender to temptation.

For popping at home, Pam offers several varieties of heartland-grown popping corns, including Baby White, Crimson Red, and Lady Fingers, each with subtle taste and texture differences. Her favorite for a striking bowl of popcorn is Black Jewell – black kernels that pop snow white. It's a tender popcorn with no hard center, said to be easier than others to digest. Follow her instructions, and you'll have the fewest unpopped kernels, called "old maids." For shake-on toppings, head on over to North Market Spices for a flavored salt, or try something a little more ambitious – combine garlic, herbs and butter for a savory, drizzle-on topping.

# "BLACK JEWELL" Popcorn
## with Garlic and Herb Butter

*makes 2 quarts*

### THE GARLIC-HERB BUTTER

| | |
|---|---|
| 4 | tablespoons butter |
| 2 | garlic cloves, peeled and minced |
| 1 | teaspoon finely-chopped fresh thyme leaves |
| 1/2 | teaspoon finely-chopped chervil leaves |
| 1/2 | teaspoon finely-chopped marjoram leaves |
| 1/2 | teaspoon finely-chopped sage sprigs |

In a small sauté pan over low heat, melt butter. Stir in garlic, sauté for 2 minutes; stir in herbs and sauté for 1 minute. Remove from heat.

### THE POPCORN

| | |
|---|---|
| 1/2 | cup Black Jewell or other popcorn kernels |
| 4 | tablespoons coconut oil |
| | garlic-herb butter (from left) |
| | popcorn salt (super-fine), to taste |

1. Heat the oil in a 3-quart covered saucepan over medium-high heat until it appears to reach a watery consistency. Add the popcorn kernels in an even layer with a pinch of salt. Gently shake the pan side to side, and when the first kernel pops, place lid on the pot, slightly off center to allow steam, but not popcorn, to escape. Continue to agitate the pot until all of the kernels have popped, about 3 minutes.

2. Remove from heat and transfer the popcorn into a wide, deep serving bowl. Just before serving, drizzle butter over the popcorn and season with salt.

# Spicy Popcorn Soup  *makes 6 servings*

**You don't have to play it straight with popcorn. Wow your guests with a piping hot bowl of soup, topped with freshly-popped popcorn serving the same purpose as croutons – adding crunch, texture, and spicy flavors to the creamy, richly-flavored bisque. There have always been plenty of reasons to love popcorn, and this unexpected dish is sure to be a showstopper.**

## THE SOUP

| | |
|---|---|
| 1 | pound large shrimp (frozen) |
| 4 | cups water |
| 3 | tablespoons olive oil |
| 2 | cups chopped onions |
| 2 | cups chopped red pepper |
| 1 | clove garlic, peeled and chopped |
| | pinch of cayenne pepper |
| 1 | ounce brandy |
| 1/2 | cup dry sherry |
| 4 | tablespoons of unsalted butter |
| 1/4 | cup all-purpose flour |
| 2 | cups half-and-half |
| | salt |
| | black pepper, freshly-cracked |

## THE POPCORN BUTTER

| | |
|---|---|
| 1/2 | cup butter |
| 1 | teaspoon red pepper flakes |
| 1 | clove garlic, minced |
| 1 | tablespoon finely-chopped chives |
| 1 | teaspoon chopped dill |
| 6 | cups popped plain popcorn |

Combine the butter, pepper flakes, and garlic, in a saucepan and place over medium-low heat until butter is melted, stirring to combine ingredients. Remove from the heat and stir in the chives and dill. Pour the mixture over the popcorn, and stir with a spatula until the popcorn is evenly coated.

**1.** In a large pot filled with 4 cups of water, place the frozen shrimp and bring to a boil over high heat. Lower the heat to a simmer, set a cover on top slightly ajar, and cook for 5 minutes. Strain and reserve the stock. Peel and devein shrimp.

**2.** Heat the olive oil in a large pot. Add the onions and red peppers and cook for 10 minutes over medium-low heat, or until the onions are tender but not browned. Add the garlic and cook 1 minute more.

**3.** Add the cayenne pepper and shrimp and cook over medium to low heat for 3 minutes, stirring occasionally. Add the brandy and cook for 1 minute, then the sherry and cook for 3 minutes longer. Transfer the shrimp and onions to a food processor and process until coarsely puréed.

**4.** In the same pot, melt the butter. Add the flour and cook over medium-low heat for 1 minute, stirring with a wooden spoon. Add the half-and-half and cook, stirring with a whisk, until thickened, about 3 minutes. Stir in the puréed shrimp, the stock, tomato paste and heat gently until hot but not boiling. Season with salt and pepper to taste.

**5.** To serve, ladle soup into 6 warmed bowls and sprinkle buttered popcorn on top of each, just before serving. Pass the bowl of remaining popcorn around the table for extra servings.

# PASTARIA

**In the words of Billy Joel,** "I'll meet you any time you want – in our Italian restaurant." And while there are no red checkered tablecloths or straw-covered Chianti bottles serving as candle-holders at Pastaria, for seekers of satisfying Italian food from an accomplished chef, this North Market fixture is as good as it gets.

The road to the eatery's success was bumpy. In 1993, when the original owner ran up a pile of bills he couldn't pay, Don Ziliak, his wholesale bread supplier, acquired Pastaria the old-fashioned way – he "inherited" it. With his background (his mother's side of the family hails from Italy), the venture wasn't much of a stretch. "I've always had a soft spot in my heart – or maybe it's in my stomach – for Italian food," admits Don.

Today, he keeps Pastaria on firm footing with the help of Rocco Valentino, a CIA-trained executive chef who earned his stripes in the kitchens of Smith & Wollensky, the Kenyon Inn, and the Granville Inn, and who brings primal Italian cooking into focus with homey, appealing dishes with some modern updates thrown in for flair.

Not surprisingly, pasta takes center stage here. Patrons are encouraged to invent their own dishes with sauces and shapes to mix and match. Choose from 16 offerings like the requisite marinara, alfredo, and pesto applications to more inventive toppings like artichoke and gorgonzola cream sauce. A Pastaria riff on rustic Southern Italian-style lasagna features thin, wide layers of pasta packed with plenty of gooey parmesan, ricotta, and mozzarella cheeses.

The kitchen turns out solid renditions of chicken and eggplant parmigiana in traditional Sicilian style. These are all smart upgrades on classics, beautifully cooked, humble Italian-American fare. *Buono appetito!*

# BLOOD ORANGE "Aperitivo"

*makes 1 drink*

In well-established Italian tradition, aperitivo drinks are made with bitter-flavored liqueurs and spirits designed to stimulate the appetite and tease the taste buds, previewing the delights of dinner. With a deliciously different take on the essential Negroni cocktail, drinksmith Travis Owens of Curio at Harvest balances bitter and sweet in his aperitivo, intensifying flavor with a "gastrique" reduction of blood oranges.

## COCKTAIL

| | |
|---|---|
| 1 1/2 | ounces Watershed Four Peel Gin |
| 1/2 | ounce Campari |
| 1/2 | ounce Cynar |
| 1/2 | ounce sweet vermouth |
| 1/2 | ounce blood orange gastrique * |
| | wedge of blood orange, for garnish |

Fill a mixing glass with ice, add gin, Campari, Cynar, vermouth, and the gastrique. Stir well and strain into rocks glass filled with fresh ice. Garnish with wedge of blood orange and serve a bowl of green olives and assorted nuts alongside.

*In a small, non-reactive saucepan, combine 1 cup sugar, ½ cup rice wine vinegar and the juice of 2 blood oranges, and bring to a boil. Reduce heat and cook over a low flame until reduced by ¾, or the mixture has thickened like a syrup. Remove from the heat and strain the mixture into a glass container. Let cool completely.*

In restaurants throughout Italy, Thursday specials are traditionally reserved for gnocchi, especially in Rome where it is customary to place a coin under the plate while eating the small dumplings to encourage prosperity. Pastaria's Chef Valentino dresses his pillow-soft potato dumplings in fresh tomato and rosemary broth. Make it on the day that you plan to serve it since gnocchi do not freeze well.

# "Thursday" Potato Gnocchi
## with Tomato-Rosemary Broth

*makes 6 servings*

### THE TOMATO ROSEMARY BROTH

| | |
|---|---|
| 1 | yellow onion, medium, diced |
| 2 | ounces garlic, chopped |
| 6 | ounces fresh rosemary, chopped |
| 28 | ounce can crushed tomatoes |
| 28 | ounces chicken or vegetale broth |
| 8 | ounces white wine |
| 1 | ounce extra virgin olive oil |
| 1 | ounce butter |

Heat olive oil and butter in sauce pan. Add onion and garlic and cook 2 to 3 minutes. Add the fresh rosemary and cook one minute. Add the wine and reduce by half. Add the crushed tomatoes and broth and simmer 45 minutes. Reserve.

1. Place potatoes in a large pot with enough water to cover. Boil the potatoes in their skins for about 40 minutes or until they can be easily pierced with a fork. Allow potatoes to cool until they can be handled. Peel the potatoes and press through a ricer or food mill fitted with a fine blade (or a fine mesh sieve). Spread the riced potatoes on a work surface and let cool completely.

2. Gather the cold riced potatoes into a mound, forming a well in the center. In a bowl, beat the eggs, salt and white pepper. Pour the egg mixture into the well. Sprinkle with nutmeg and work the potatoes and eggs together with both hands. Gradually add 3 cups of the flour and scrape the dough up from the work surface with a knife as often as necessary. Add the grated cheese. (Incorporation of the ingredients should take no longer than 10 minutes. The longer the dough is worked, the more flour it will require and the heavier it will become).

## THE GNOCCHI

| | |
|---|---|
| 6 | large Idaho or russet potatoes |
| I | teaspoon salt |
| 1/2 | teaspoon white pepper, freshly-ground |
| 2 | eggs, beaten |
| 4 | cups flour |
| 1/2 | cup grated Parmigiano-Reggiano cheese |
| | pinch of nutmeg |
| 6 | sprigs rosemary, for garnish |
| | tomato-rosemary broth (from left) |

3. Dust the dough, your hands, and the work surface lightly with flour. Cut the dough into six equal parts and set aside. Work one piece of dough. Continue to dust dough, hands, and surface as long as the dough feels sticky.

4. Using both hands, roll the piece of dough into a rope ½" thick, then slice the rope at ½" intervals. Sprinkle some flour and roll each piece into a ball, flouring as needed. Place on a lightly-oiled sheet pan and continue until all dough is finished.

5. To cook the gnocchi, bring 6 quarts of well-salted water to a boil. Drop the gnocchi into the boiling water a few at a time, stirring gently with a wooden spoon, and cook for about 90 seconds from the time they rise to the surface. Remove the cooked gnocchi with a skimmer and shake off the excess water. As soon as all the gnocchi are ready, divide into 6 warmed pasta bowls, pour heated broth over them, garnish each with a sprig of rosemary, and serve immediately.

# Pure Imagination CHOCOLATIER

**"Imagination is everything,"** Albert Einstein once said. "It is the preview of life's coming attractions." When Daniel Cooper left behind a desk job to launch Pure Imagination, it was the fulfillment of a lifelong dream.

His fascination with confections began in the kitchen of his grandparents' restaurant, the old Biltmore in the Hilltop neighborhood of Columbus. He can look back on how his youthful love of "anything chocolate" grew into a period of research and experimentation while he worked at multiple jobs to save enough money to make a business of it. In 2001, Daniel was ready to transform himself into a professional chocolatier when a space was offered to him at the North Market.

His efforts begin with dark, untempered couverture chocolate from a Swiss firm that employs judges to taste and evaluate the most intensely-flavored fair trade cacao beans from South America and Africa. Each voluptuous creation is rolled, cut, dipped and decorated by human hands in small batches.

"Chocolatiers are best known for their truffles," says Daniel. "They are the diamonds of the chocolate world, which is why we take such pride in them." He not only dreams up intriguing flavor combinations, but he perfectly executes those dreams into irresistible treats. His face lights up as he describes one of his imaginative pairings – fresh blueberry puree with a gouda ganache cream. "There is just something special about the two flavors together," he says. "I don't know what it is or how to put it in words, but it just sings to me."

Daniel believes that his fine chocolates deserve to be matched up with the best ingredients. "I am really careful in selecting components that are real standouts and make my pieces shine," he explains. He favors local strawberries in season, local wildflower honey, as well as nuts and freshly-ground peanut butter from Krema – just up the street from the Market.

Its name refers to the cacao tree native to the deep tropical region of South America whose seeds are used to make chocolate. Daniel's "Theobrama" truffles borrow from the ancient Mayan practice of adding cayenne to the pulverized, roasted, and melted-down by-product of their treasured cacao beans, while the addition of nutmeg adds a sweet and mildly-bitter dimension for complexity and depth of flavor. The truffles provide inspiration for a sensual hot chocolate with flavors that surround the palate like a warm embrace. (Note: Once ground, nutmeg will quickly lose its fragrance and flavor, so you are best off buying it in its whole form and grinding as you go).

# "Theobroma" Hot Chocolate
# with Cayenne Whipped Cream

*makes 1 serving*

### THE WHIPPED CREAM

| | |
|---|---|
| 1 | cup heavy cream |
| 2 | tablespoons confectioner's sugar, or to taste |
| 1/2 | teaspoon vanilla extract |
| | pinch cayenne pepper |

Add the cream to mixing bowl and whip until the cream is slightly thickened. Add the sugar, vanilla, and cayenne, and continue whipping until cream holds its shape.

### THE HOT CHOCOLATE

| | |
|---|---|
| 8 | ounces whole milk |
| 1/4 | teaspoon ground cayenne pepper |
| 1/4 | teaspoon nutmeg |
| 4 | ounces dark bittersweet chocolate, finely chopped |
| 1 | teaspoon confectioner's sugar, or to taste |
| | cayenne whipped cream (from left) |

Heat the milk with cayenne and nutmeg to just under a boil. Add the chocolate and stir continuously with a wooden spoon until fully melted. Add the sugar and stir until combined. Remove from heat and allow the blended liquid to steep for 10 minutes. Return to heat and bring gently back to a simmer. Spoon whipped cream on top and serve.

# SAREFINO'S

**Make no mistake:** For honest-to-goodness New York-style pizza, beloved by people of all ages and revered for its taste, toppings and foldability, head on over to Sarefino's, a long-time bulwark at the North Market. The pizzeria was founded in 1990 by Long Island native Linda Gemelli and named for her uncle who supplied the original recipes. Then in 1995, Sarefino's was purchased by Don Ziliak, operator of Pastaria (see page 104), strategically consolidating the Italian eateries and becoming "Godfather" of the Market.

## PIZZERIA AND ITALIAN DELI

Devotees of New York pizza say forgetaboutit – there's no other way to make a pie. It's got to be hand-tossed so the crust is crisp in the center, chewy around the edge and foldable (people from New York fold their pizza in half and then eat it). Tomato sauce and stringy mozzarella cheese are essential, and the trick at Sarefino's is deciding on other toppings. Favorites include pepperoni, cheese, and a mouth-watering veggie pizza with spinach, artichokes, and roasted red peppers.

Badda bing, badda boom! True to New York street-food culture, Sarefino's pizza is offered by the slice or as a whole pie. The large pie, typically around 16 inches in diameter, is commonly cut into 6 slices, and that's a big slice-a-pizza! You'll need a knife and fork (and a few napkins) for a Sarefino's calzone, while its street-food cousin, the stromboli, can be devoured on the go.

Don admits that he enjoys the daily parade of customers, and he compares Sarefino's to the family pizza parlor back in the old days. "A parlor is where people gather to talk," he says, "a place where people where people connect with friends and neighbors – to me, that's the North Market."

# DINO'S "Flame of Love"

*makes 1 drink*

When the moon hits your eye like a bigga pizza pie, that's a perfect occasion for the "Flame of Love," a cocktail created for Steubenville, Ohio native Dean Martin in 1970 by Pepe Ruiz, bartender at Chasen's in West Hollywood. For your next pizza party, show off your skills at both mixology and pyrotechnics, as well as your allegiance to locally-distilled vodka.

## COCKTAIL

| | |
|---|---|
| 1/2 | ounce Fino sherry |
| 2 | orange peel medallions (the size of a 50¢ piece) |
| 2 | ounces Watershed vodka |

1. Add the sherry to a pre-chilled martini glass, swirl to coat completely, and discard the excess. Stir the vodka with ice in a cocktail shaker to chill, then fine-strain into the coated glass.

2. Using a long wooden match, express and ignite the oils from the orange medallions a few inches above the drink, oily skin toward the flame, one at a time.

3. Discard the first medallion, drop the second one into the drink and serve..

# Pizzeria "ROCKET" Salad

*makes 4 servings*

The pizzaiolo flips and stretches and shapes the dough and adds the toppings; the fornino wields the long-handled peel to transfer the pizza to the oven. Any way you slice it, the amalgam of cheese, sauce, and crust is dish that makes people happy when they eat it. With a sharp bite to cleanse the palate, arugula (or roquette) is the requisite choice of greens to accompany family pizza night.

## SALAD

| | |
|---|---|
| 1 | bunch arugula, trimmed |
| 8 | ounces mixed baby greens |
| 16 | grape tomatoes, cut in half lengthwise |
| 1/2 | cup pine nuts, toasted |
| 3 | tablespoons extra virgin olive oil |
| 1 | tablespoon balsamic vinegar |
| | sea salt |
| | black pepper, freshly-cracked |
| | parmesan cheese, shaved with a potato peeler |

1. Place arugula and mixed greens in a serving bowl. Add tomatoes and pine nuts, and toss well. In small bowl, mix together oil, vinegar, and salt and pepper to taste. Just before serving, pour over salad and toss well.

2. To serve, pass salad bowl family-style around the table, passing the parmesan shavings alongside.

**In 1892, leaving behind the daily hardships in Sucha, Hungary,** Nathan Wasserstrom arrived in America with the expectation of a better life. Five years later, while working in New York's garment district, he married Rebecca Rosenberg, and in 1902 they re-settled in Columbus

Like many immigrants, Nathan became a peddler, selling sundries from a horse-pulled wagon along the well-traveled city streets. At night he worked as a bartender on North High Street, and once he saved up enough money he was able to purchase the business – just as passage of the 18th amendment prepared to prohibit the sale of alcoholic beverages. Undeterred, Nathan converted the bar into a supply store, and with a wink and a nod, began selling malt extract, hops, bottles, other supplies for home brew. Over the following decade, he added nine branch stores throughout the city.

With the lifting of Prohibition, Nathan and his ambitious sons expanded into wholesale wines, restaurant fixtures, supplies, and equipment. Family has always been at the center of the enterprise, and by the time Rodney Wasserstrom joined the firm as part of its third generation in the early 1950s, the company had emerged as one of the nation's fastest growing suppliers to the food service industry.

"When the Market moved from the Quonset hut and re-opened in the new space, we knew we wanted to do something there – something that connected to our roots in the community," says Rodney. "We began selling our company's returns and overstock at discounted prices."

"Over the years, offerings have expanded to include commercial restaurant supplies, china, glassware, cooking and serving ware, even chef coats," explains Rodney. "If you're one of those cooks who wants their home kitchen to look and feel more like a restaurant kitchen, we're here to help."

# THE source
## BY wasserstrom

"A good starting knife set would be a wide-blade chef's knife, pairing knife, and boning knife," advises Rodney Wasserstrom. "With these knives you can do most kitchen cutting. It's very important to have the right knife for the job." At Hubbard Grille, Chef Drew Thompson employs a large chef's knife to chop, chop, chop and turn, turn, turn to mix, mix, mix. In his well-made chopped salad, all the ingredients are uniform in size and every bite is a confetti-burst of flavor. You can prepare much of it ahead of time, and then assemble the salad at the last minute. Serve each portion with a thick slice of crusty bread with butter.

# Chop Chop Salad with Chimichurri

*makes 4 servings*

## THE CHIMICHURRI

| | |
|---|---|
| 1 | cup cilantro stems and leaves, rinsed and dried |
| 1 | cup parsley stems and leaves, rinsed and dried |
| 2 | tablespoons minced garlic cloves |
| 3/4 | cup extra virgin olive oil |
| 1/4 | cup red wine vinegar |
| | juice of 1 lime |
| 1/2 | teaspoon black pepper, freshly-cracked |
| | pinch of salt |

Run a wide-blade chef's knife back and forth across the cilantro and parsley, chopping finely (use a very sharp knife that will cut, rather than crush, the herbs). In a medium bowl, whisk together garlic olive oil, vinegar, lime juice, pepper and salt. Whisk in herbs. Set aside until ready to use.

## THE SALAD

| | |
|---|---|
| 1 | romaine lettuce heart |
| 1 | cup shredded cabbage |
| 4 | slices smoked bacon, cooked until crisp, cooled, and chopped |
| 1 | heirloom tomato, diced |
| 1 | Granny Smith apple, diced |
| | chimichurri (from left) |
| | sea salt |
| | black pepper, freshly-cracked |
| 1 | cup crumbled Maytag blue cheese |

1. With a wide-blade chef's knife, chop the lettuce heart into ½" pieces. Combine it with the bacon, other vegetables in a large bowl and toss the mixture well.

2. Keep the salad chilled until ready to serve. Then toss it again with enough chimichurri to lightly coat the vegetables, and season with salt and pepper to taste.

3. To serve, layer salad on 4 chilled plates, and divide and sprinkle the blue cheese over the top of each. Serve at once, passing any extra chimichurri alongside.

# taste of BELGIUM

**His foray into the North Market comes naturally** to Jean-François Flechet. He grew up in a small village near Liège, the Eastern Belgian city where locals gather at weekly markets and beguiling street fairs for a local treat called *gaufres de chasse* or "Hunting Waffles."

He came to the U.S. to study economics at the University of Pennsylvania, moved to Cincinnati, and after a stint in the corporate world, began developing the prototype for a high-tech hot food vending machine. When funds ran out, Jean-François needed a way to support the project as he searched for investors, and a trip back home to visit family inspired a big idea. He returned with a 120-pound, deep-pocket waffle iron, set it up at the back of a produce stand at Cincinnati's Findlay Market, and began serving his hometown specialty.

What they are not, oddly enough, are what most of us think of as Belgian waffles. These are uniquely Liège waffles, expertly made from a richer, yeast-based dough, compared to traditional pancake-type batter. Customary Belgian sugar is thoroughly mixed in, and when heated between the honeycombed cast iron plates, the coarse pieces caramelize, producing a crispy exterior and leaving the center soft, chewy, and delicately warm.

Flushed with success, he put the vending machine into storage and in 2009 installed a second base of operations at the North Market. Here, in Liège tradition, waffles are dusted with powdered sugar and sold in waxed wrappers as a snack – portable and easy to eat while walking and shopping.

As supporting players, Jean-Francois offers sweet and savory crêpes, salads and locally-roasted espresso drinks. Sweet varieties include caramel au beurre salé (lightly salted French caramel) and lavender sugar with freshly squeezed lemon. These are the kind of things that make you start planning your next visit.

Besides indulgent waffles, the region of Liège is known for a slightly acidic salad of green beans, potatoes, and ham, eaten warm or at room temperature. It can be a starter, but is most often served as a main course, especially popular during the autumn months. Like all regional dishes, it has as many variations, including the addition of a poached egg or quarters of a hard-boiled egg. As they say in Liège, *Mangez bien, riez souvent, aimez beaucoup*, which means "Eat well, laugh often, love abundantly."

# Salade Liègeoise *makes 4 servings*

## MAIN DISH

| | |
|---|---|
| 1 | pound green beans, trimmed and cut in half |
| 4 | large red potatoes |
| 1 | large onion, chopped |
| 1/3 | cup diced chives |
| 1/2 | pound Canadian-style bacon |
| 1/2 | cup red wine vinegar |
| | salt |
| | black pepper, freshly-cracked |

**1.** Boil potatoes (with skins on) in lightly salted water until cooked through but still firm. Remove, peel and slice to about ¼" thickness and place in warm serving bowl. Boil green beans until just cooked but still firm (al dente). Drain well and add to the bowl.

**2.** Cut bacon into small squares and cook in skillet over medium-high heat until crispy. Sprinkle bacon over salad, reserving ⅓ cup of cooking fat. Pour fat over salad. Place skillet back on burner and pour in vinegar. Bring to boil, then pour over salad.

**3.** Sprinkle onion and chives over salad, season with salt and pepper to taste, and toss well in a chilled bowl.

**4.** To serve, pass the salad bowl around the table, family-style.

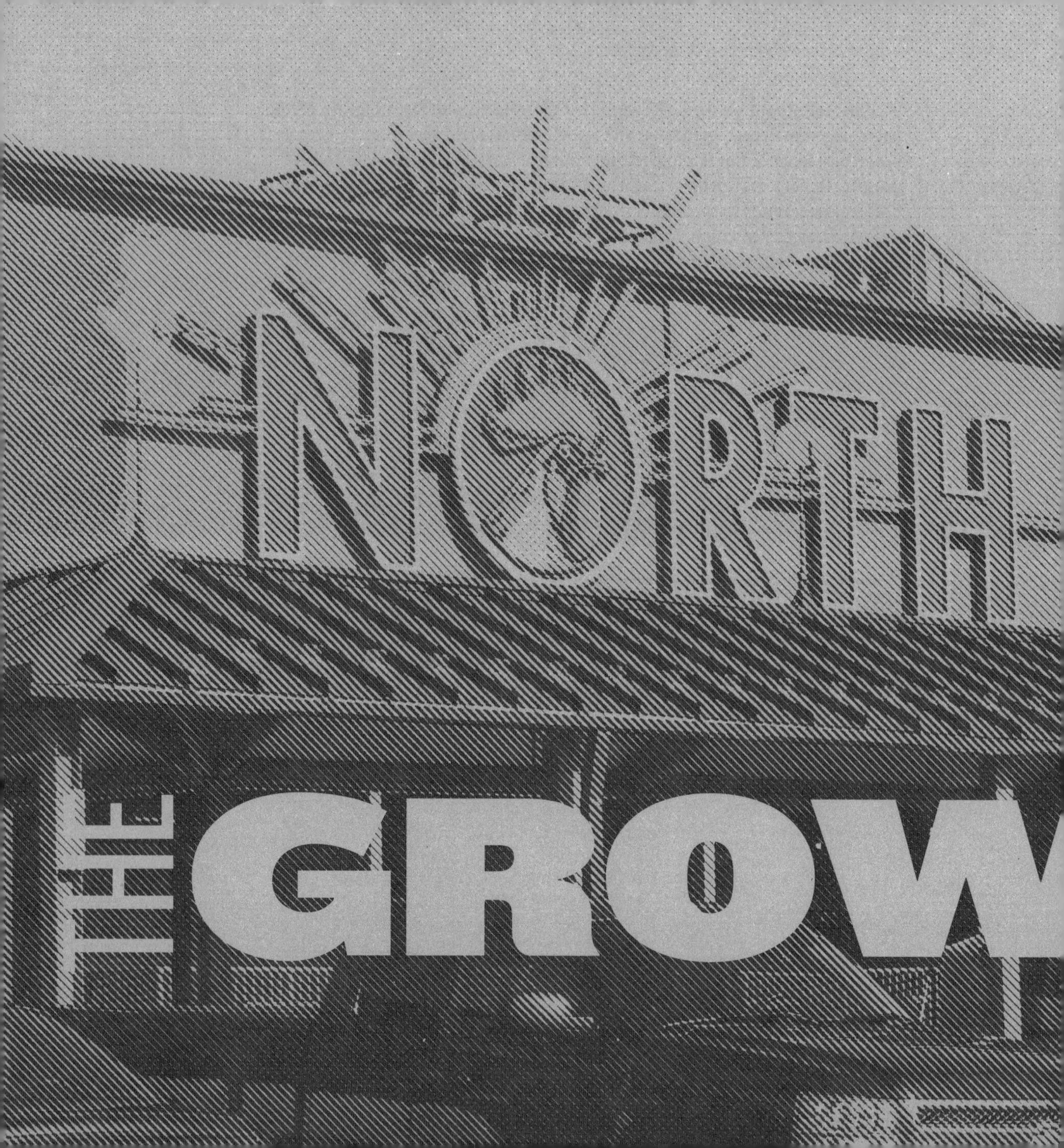
NORTH
THE GROW

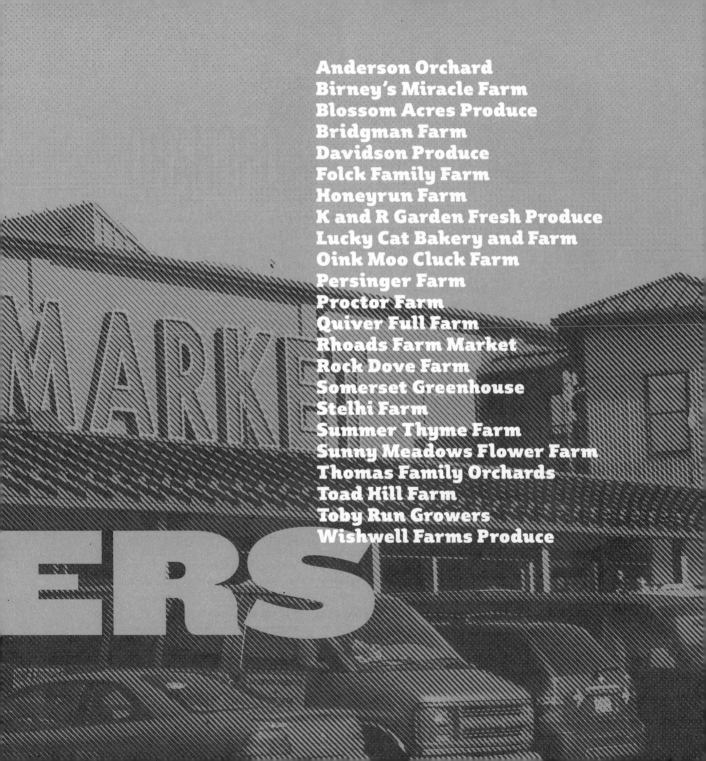

Anderson Orchard
Birney's Miracle Farm
Blossom Acres Produce
Bridgman Farm
Davidson Produce
Folck Family Farm
Honeyrun Farm
K and R Garden Fresh Produce
Lucky Cat Bakery and Farm
Oink Moo Cluck Farm
Persinger Farm
Proctor Farm
Quiver Full Farm
Rhoads Farm Market
Rock Dove Farm
Somerset Greenhouse
Stelhi Farm
Summer Thyme Farm
Sunny Meadows Flower Farm
Thomas Family Orchards
Toad Hill Farm
Toby Run Growers
Wishwell Farms Produce

# ANDERSON ORCHARD

**"Farming appealed to me,** as it probably appeals to other people, because it's simple and straightforward work outdoors with literal fruits from your labor," says Steve Anderson, a high school science teacher-turned-grower. "I just didn't know how hard it would be."

The venture became a reality in 1985. "My wife Judy and I jumped right in with an apple orchard and a strawberry farm," he explains, "but we planted too much for two people to take care of and too little to earn a living." Along the way, they learned what works for them and for their land – it was neither apples nor strawberries. "Our journey is always evolving," says Steve. "The nature of small scale farming demands flexibility and the willingness to change."

The Andersons were drawn to perennial asparagus, a high value specialty crop and the earliest producing spring vegetable. The first plantings were "Mary Washington," a strong-growing and productive variety producing long, thick spears, then a disease-resistant variety called Jersey Giant, prized for its bright green color and flavorful spears. Asparagus shows up at the Market as early as the last week in April. "It's one of the few things you grow that people actually get really excited about," says Steve. "Folks that like it, really like it."

Other crops include tomatoes, corn, leeks, beans, as well as figs and "Olympics," sweetest of the Asian pear varieties. In order to "fill in the gaps" between harvests, Steve and Judy bring farm-grown cut flowers to the Market, fragrant peonies in mid-May and big, beautiful sunflowers in late June.

"Besides providing a venue for our offerings, the North Market is a social experience," says Steve, "something we look forward to every week. You get to know the folks you're selling to, pretty well in some cases."

Columbus in springtime is an edible city. That's when Chef Connor O'Neill puts a Mezzo kitchen spin on a traditional condiment from Italy's Lombardy region. While lemon, parsley and garlic are typical ingredients, Connor enhances the mixture with chili flakes, sharp Italian cheese, and orange and lemon juices. "If you find plain vegetables to be boring, add gremolata," suggests the chef, who imparts a striking complexity of flavors in this ode to a springtime delicacy, and serves it as accompaniment to local spring lamb.

# Asparagus "GREMOLATA"

*makes 4–6 servings*

## GREMOLATA

| | |
|---|---|
| 1/2 | orange |
| 2 | garlic cloves, minced |
| 1/4 | cup finely-chopped parsley |
| 1 | teaspoon chili flakes |
| 1 | tablespoon sharp dry cheese (Pecorino or super-firm Manchego), grated |
| 2 | pounds asparagus, trimmed |
| | salt |
| | black pepper, freshly-cracked |
| 1 | tablespoon fresh orange juice |
| 1 | tablespoon fresh lemon juice |
| 2 | tablespoons extra virgin olive oil |

**1.** Using vegetable peeler, remove peel in long strips from the orange. Mince orange peel. Combine orange peel, garlic, parsley, chili flakes, and cheese in a bowl.

**2.** Boil the asparagus in well-salted water until tender, four to five minutes. Remove from the heat, and toss with the gremolata. Season with salt and pepper to taste.

**3.** To serve, transfer the asparagus to a warmed serving platter. Mix together the orange juice, lemon juice and olive oil, and drizzle over the asparagus. Pass family-style around the table.

"Asparagus inspires gentle thoughts," wrote English poet Charles Lamb. The first asparagus to arrive at the Market becomes the centerpiece of a salad that "tastes like Spring," created by Chef Bill Glover for the Gallerie Bar and Bistro. Harbingers of the season, asparagus is said to be full of "chi," the Chinese word for life force. The salad is delicious with a poached egg on top; the yolk becomes part of its dressing.

# "Earth Day" Salad
## with Asparagus and Poached Egg

*makes 4 servings*

## THE SALAD

| | |
|---|---|
| 1 | bunch asparagus |
| 2 | bunches Belgium endive |
| 4 | local free range eggs |
| 1 | fresh black truffle (2 ounces) |
| 4 | ounces smoked slab bacon, cut into lardons and rendered |
| 4 | ounces ricotta salata |
| | balsamic vinaigrette (from below) |

## THE VINAIGRETTE

| | |
|---|---|
| 2 | ounces balsamic vinegar |
| 6 | ounces extra virgin olive oil |
| 1 | teaspoon Dijon mustard |
| 1 | tablespoon freshly chopped tarragon |
| 1 | teaspoon kosher salt |
| 1/4 | teaspoon white pepper |

Place all of the ingredients in a blender and blend on high until emulsified.

**1.** Trim the bottom two inches off of the asparagus and peel the lower half of the stalk. Lightly oil the asparagus and season with salt and pepper to taste. Grill the spears over medium high heat until lightly charred.

**2.** Split the Belgium endive lengthwise and lightly dress them with the vinaigrette and season the cut heads of lettuce. Roast them cut side down in an oven set at 425° F. for 15 minutes.

**3.** Cut the slab bacon into ¼" x ¼" x 1" lardons and render in a dry pan over medium high heat until crispy yet tender inside.

**4.** Poach the eggs in a sauce pot containing 2 quarts of water with two tablespoons of white vinegar. Bring the water bath to 200° F., slip the cracked whole eggs into the poaching liquid for about 3 to 5 minutes. (You want the eggs white to be set while the yolk will begin to thicken but not hard). Remove the eggs with a slotted spoon and drain on a towel in the spoon.

**5.** To serve, place roasted endive on the center of each of 4 plates, lay grilled asparagus over the top. Spoon a seasoned poached egg onto each salad. Drizzle the vinaigrette over each plate, then shave the ricotta salata and black truffle over the eggs and serve.

# BIRNEY'S MIRACLE FARM

**Every successful enterprise is, in a way, a small miracle. After thirty years of growing vegetables and selling from a small open-air stand on their farm, Richard and Bonnie Birney passed along the family tradition to their daughter Caren and her husband Eric Conkey.**

"My folks decided to call the farm 'Miracle,'" explains Caren, "because no matter what the weather – flood, drought, hailstorm, whatever – a divine miracle always seemed to insure that we would have a crop to sell, even extra to donate to our local food pantry."

Originally a cattle farm, the Birneys started planting sweet corn for the family's own consumption, and according to Caren, "It was so good, we thought maybe we should sell it. Before long, we were growing corn, tomatoes, green beans, and cucumbers, and selling from our front yard and offering u-pick." But the farm has gone on to make a name for itself with peppers, and in fact now harvests nearly 50,000 pepper plants every season.

"People really like the versatility of peppers," says Caren. "They are great flavoring agents when you add them to your cooking. You can choose all kinds of different varieties to get different combinations of flavor and heat." Their varying degrees of heat come from capsaicin, a chemical compound concentrated in the internal membrane of the plants where the seeds are attached. The farm grows the widest varieties of peppers in the state, ranging from sweet to mild to incendiary. "Initially, we started with bell peppers and banana peppers, and branched out from there," explains Caren. "When someone asked if we could grow something hotter, we decided to try other varieties. We're now growing Bhut Jolokias and Moruga Scorpions for John Hard of CaJohn's Firey Foods.'

In the words of G. K. Chesterson, "The most incredible thing about miracles is that they happen."

# Seared Scallops
## with Hot Pepper Cream

*makes 4 servings*

Versatile and flavor-friendly, scallops pair well with whatever surrounding you choose. In this combination of textures and succulent flavors, an aggressive kick from the hot peppers contrasts with the gentle sweetness of the scallops. There are distinctive heat levels in the wide choice of peppers, so you will want to experiment with different peppers from Birney's each time you prepare this dish. For a finishing touch, season with a smidgen of lemon-dill flavored salt from North Market Spices.

### MAIN DISH

| | |
|---|---|
| 16 | large sea scallops |
| 2 | tablespoons fresh-squeezed lime juice |
| | salt |
| | black pepper, freshly-cracked |
| 2 | tablespoons olive oil |
| 1 – 2 | jalapeño or other hot peppers, including seeds, finely-chopped |
| 1/2 | cup heavy cream |
| | pinch of "Aqua" lemon-dill salt |
| | chopped fresh cilantro, for garnish |

1. Rinse the scallops and place in a large bowl along with the lime juice and season with salt and pepper to taste. Cover and refrigerate for 1 to 2 hours (no longer or scallops will "cook"). Remove from the marinade and pat dry.

2. Heat the olive oil in a heavy skillet over medium-high heat. Add scallops and sear on one side, about 2 minutes; turn scallops over with tongs or spatula and sear the other side, 1 to 2 minutes more. Transfer to a warm plate and pour off oil left in the pan.

3. Return the pan to medium heat and add the peppers. Stir to brown slightly, about 1 minute. Reduce heat to low, stir in the cream and bring to a simmer.

4. To serve, ladle a portion of sauce onto 4 warmed dinner plates and arrange 4 scallops on top of each. Add a pinch of the flavored salt and scatter chopped cilantro over each serving.

Goodness gracious! It's a tantalizing sauce laced with chiles ground into a smooth paste along with garlic, named after the city of Sri Racha in Thailand, and it puts the finishing touch on an irreverent coleslaw devised by Chef Tonya Harris of Dirty Franks Hot Dog Palace. "Sriracha isn't just a sauce that people like a lot," says Tonya, "it's something that people are seriously obsessed with."

# Cilantro-Jalapeño "HOT MESS" with Sriracha

*makes 6 servings*

## SALAD

| | |
|---|---|
| 3 | cups mayonnaise |
| 1 | jalapeño pepper, roasted, finely-diced * |
| 1 | bunch cilantro, cleaned and chopped |
| 2 | tablespoons white vinegar |
| 1 1/2 | teaspoons celery seeds |
| 1/4 | cup sugar |
| 2 | teaspoons salt |
| 3/4 | teaspoon black pepper, freshly-cracked |
| 1/4 | teaspoon cayenne |
| 4 | cups finely-chopped green cabbage |
| 1/4 | cup shredded carrots |
| | sriracha, for drizzle |

1. In a medium bowl, mix together mayonnaise, jalapeno, cilantro, vinegar, celery seeds, sugar, salt, pepper, and cayenne until well blended. Taste for seasoning. Add cabbage and carrots. Blend well and refrigerate for 1 hour.

2. Serve family-style from a bowl or divide among 6 salad plates. Pass sriracha around the table for drizzling, according to individual taste preferences.

* Cut the pepper in half and remove the stem, veins, and seeds. Coat lightly with oil and, using metal tongs, place the flesh of the pepper as close to the flame of the broiler as possible and rotate until the skin blackens and blisters. Remove from the heat, let it cool, and scrape off the blackened skin. Remove and discard the seed pod, stem and inner ribs before using.

# Poblano Escobar

*makes 1 drink*

From Travis Owens' mind comes shrewd handiwork. The Curio at Harvest drink-smith demonstrates how local peppers add layers of flavor complexity to what he calls a "ground to glass" cocktail. Birney's Miracle Farm provides mildly-hot poblanos for juicing and very, very hot red habañeros to infuse the agave sweetener.

## COCKTAIL

| | |
|---|---|
| 1 | ounce mezcal |
| 1/2 | ounce tequila |
| 3/4 | ounce fresh poblano juice |
| 3/4 | ounce freshly-squeezed lime |
| 1/4 | ounce red habañero-infused agave nectar* |
| 1/2 | Cointreau or other orange liqueur |
| | alderwood-smoked salt |
| | fresh lime wheel, for garnish |

1. Combine mescal, tequila, poblano juice, lime, infused agave, and Cointreau with ice in a shaker. Shake vigorously.

2. Rim a pre-chilled Old Fashioned cocktail glass by moistening the edge with a lime wedge, then dipping the glass into a small plate of the smoked salt.

3. Double-strain into the glass, and garnish with the lime wheel.

*Thinly slice 2 habañero peppers and place in a non-reactive container with 1 cup of agave nectar. Let sit for 1 hour at room temperature, agitating every 15 minutes. Strain peppers and seeds through cheese cloth, making sure to give a good squeeze. This infusion can be made based upon tolerance to heat. If it gets too hot, dilute with more agave nectar. (Make sure to wear gloves during the process).*

# blossom acres

**Discipline, hard work, and love of the soil** are essential to farming, qualities that are synonymous with Amish culture and traditions. The Amish are some of the best farmers in the world.

Eli Yoder describes his farm as thirty acres of bottom land with fourteen inches of topsoil and an excellent source of irrigation from a creek that runs alongside. "It's an appealing place to grow vegetables," he says of Blossom Acres, located in the Amish village of Millersburg along the rolling hills of east-central Ohio.

Amish farming skills are passed down by ancestors, from generation to generation, with fathers teaching sons, much as an apprentice would learn from a craftsman. "We don't use pesticides, herbicides, or chemicals," explains Eli. "As a farmer, I understand my responsibility to maintain nutrients in the soil. My main focus is soil health – healthy soil and healthy people go hand in hand."

In keeping with his religious, family and community values, Eli has chosen to do without some of the technology that other farmers use. His two Percheron horses, a sound breed known for their spirit and beauty, are used for plough-ing and harvesting instead of tractors. "Their names are Bob and Dan," he says. "We have a close bond with them."

Among his eighty-eight different vegetables, Eli has a few favorites. "Merlins" are the sweetest among beet varieties, with great color, flavor and uniformity; "Yukon Gold" potatoes have beautiful golden color and savory, creamy potato flavor; cold-hardy greens including Swiss chard, arugula, mizuna, and kale are prolific in his rich soil. But his best sellers at the Market are the gorgeous white "Candy" onions, a hybrid variety that grows big and very sweet – sweeter than Vidalias. According to Eli, "I enjoy raising something good for people to eat – these onions are really, really good."

PRODUCE

"Every oven will be different," explains Chef Peter Chapman of The Pearl. "Remove the kale before it turns brown, but after it dries out. In the Pearl kitchen we cook it for different amounts of time depending on the oven – in one it takes five minutes, in another it takes seven, and in the third it takes about four minutes – so you will have to experiment." Using his simple instructions, the kale is not masked by other flavors or cooking methods; leaves turn from a dusty dark green to dark emerald with curly edges that crunch. This vegetable side dish is should be served hot from the oven; leaves lose their crisp texture as the dish stands.

# Crispy Oven-Roasted Kale

*makes 4–6 servings*

## SIDE DISH

| | |
|---|---|
| 1 | pound kale |
| 2 | tablespoons canola oil or as needed |
| | kosher salt |

1. Pull the stiff stem out of the center of the kale, rinse under cold water, and spin dry. Get some oil on your fingers and rub the kale until all parts of it are shiny. Season sparingly with salt.

2. Place on a parchment-lined sheet tray and bake at 450° F. until crispy. Remove the kale from the oven.

3. To serve, transfer to a warmed bowl and pass family-style around the table.

"Some vegetables are persistently underestimated," writes Tamar Adler of the onion. Although some enthusiasts insist that Candy Onions can be eaten like an apple, most prefer them in a dish like this sweet, warming caramelized soup, thick enough to stand a spoon. This no-cliché version by Chef Brian Cook of the Columbus Brewing Company is distinguished by the hoppy aromatics of India Pale Ale, providing instant aromatherapy at the local fall and winter table.

# I.P.A. "Candy Onion" Soup

*makes 4 servings*

## SOUP

| | |
|---|---|
| 6 | tablespoons unsalted butter |
| 1 1/2 | pounds candy onions, peeled and thinly sliced |
| 1 | leek, cleaned and diced |
| 1 | shallot, peeled and diced |
| 3 1/2 | cups chicken broth |
| 1/2 | cup sherry |
| 1/2 | cup Marsala wine |
| 1 | cup Columbus Beer Company I.P.A. |
| 1 | teaspoon brown sugar |
| | salt |
| | black pepper, freshly-cracked |
| 4 | slices whole grain bread, toasted |
| 1 | cup coarsely-grated Oakville Farmstead or other Gouda-style cheese |
| | chopped fresh chives, for garnish |

1. Melt butter in a medium soup pot over medium-high heat. Add onions, leeks, and shallots, and sauté until soft and light brown, about 10 minutes. Stir in the chicken broth, sherry, Marsala, ale, and brown sugar. Reduce to just under a boil, and season with salt and pepper to taste. Simmer uncovered, for 20 to 30 minutes.

2. Ladle soup into 4 ovenproof bowls. Place toasted bread over liquid and sprinkle ¼ cup of the cheese onto each slice. Place under pre-heated broiler and heat until the cheese melts to a crispy brown, about 3 minutes. Allow to cool slightly, and add a sprinkling of chives over each just before serving.

# Amish Farmstead Potatoes
## with Onions, Peppers, and Garlic

*makes 4–6 servings*

In the early 1900s, Dutch and Belgian immigrants began vegetable farming along the Canadian shore of Lake Erie. In the 1950s, regional vegetable growers began petitioning for the breeding rights and licensing for a gold-fleshed potato variety they were used to growing in Europe, inspiring the development of Yukon Gold by the Ontario Agriculture College at the University of Guelph. Big, early, great-tasting Yukon Golds are starchy enough to bake and firm enough to boil, in Eli's words, "as close to the everything potato as exists."

## SIDE DISH

| | |
|---|---|
| 2 | pounds Yukon Gold potatoes |
| 2 | large red peppers |
| 2 | large green peppers |
| 3 | large red onions, cut into thin wedges |
| 6 | garlic cloves, thinly sliced |
| 6 | bay leaves |
| | leaves from 4 large thyme sprigs |
| 6 | tablespoons olive oil |
| | salt |
| | black pepper, freshly-cracked |

1. Preheat the oven to 400° F. Bring a large pan of well-salted water to a boil. Cut the potatoes across into ¼"-thick slices, drop them into the water, bring back to a boil and cook for 1 or 2 minutes or until just tender.

2. Halve the red and green peppers, remove and discard the stalks and seeds. Cut into ¼"-wide strips and place into a large roasting pan with the potatoes, onions, garlic, bay leaves and thyme leaves. Season with salt and pepper to taste, and toss well with 4 tablespoons of the olive oil. Spread out in a single layer and drizzle over the remainder of the oil.

3. Roast on the top shelf of the oven for 15 minutes, then remove the pan and turn the vegetables over. Return to the oven and roast for a further 15 minutes, until potatoes are golden and the other vegetables are tender. Remove from the oven.

4. Transfer to a large warmed serving bowl and serve family-style around the table.

# BRIDGMAN farm

**Nearly thirty years ago,** Mary Bridgman, a reporter for the *Columbus Dispatch*, started her own small patch of organic vegetables on a rented 20-by-20 foot plot on the OSU campus. Before long, she outgrew the small plot of vegetables and transitioned from gardener to farmer with the purchase of a 43-acre farm in the Licking County village of Johnstown. By the early 1990s she was selling her produce at the Worthington Farmers Market.

She farmed part-time for next several years, re-settling on a 67-acre spread in Washington Court House, nearly halfway between Columbus and Cincinnati, expanding sales to the North Market in 1997. Ten years later, she left the newsroom behind, as Bridgman Farm became a full-time endeavor. "It's not something you plan, there's not a 'eureka' moment," she says. "It just sort of happens – you enjoy what you're doing and it makes sense to keep doing more."

She calls tomatoes her specialty crop, and marketgoers love the rainbow of colors in her mixed pints of cherry tomatoes. "Kellogg's Breakfast is my favorite big heirloom variety," says Mary. Originally bred in Michigan by a grower named Kellogg, it is absolutely unique, both for its size and wonderful texture."

The intrepid Ms. Bridgman coaxes many other things from the earth, including lettuces, greens, roots, peas, cucumbers, peppers, eggplant, turnips, kohlrabi, zucchini, and lots of onions – 20,000 to be exact. "Folks who go to the Market are savvy and discriminating," she explains. They understand the importance of local agriculture; they know what they're looking for, and they keep you on your toes."

"Farming is a great life, a healthy life," says Mary. "It's a lot of hard work, but there are many rewards – like when someone says 'your vegetables are beautiful!' It just makes my head swell."

Because the colors (red tomato, white onion, and green jalapeño) are reminiscent of the Mexican flag, the dish is called salsa bandera (flag salad). "The flavor of heirlooms is far superior to the bland grocery store tomatoes I grew up with," says Chef Keith Adams of Tip Top Kitchen and Cocktails. When local varieties start rolling into the Market, Keith goes to work with a sharp knife on the chopping block. For his potent version of *pico de gallo*, he leaves in the seeds and ribs of the pepper, but you may remove them to mellow out the heat and still deliver their flavor.

# Heirloom Tomato "Salsa Bandara"

*makes 6 servings*

## SALSA

| | |
|---|---|
| 2 | large, ripe heirloom tomatoes, seeded and cored, finely-diced |
| 1 | jalapeño pepper, minced (seeds and ribs optional) |
| 1 | small red onion, finely-diced |
| 1/2 | cup minced cilantro |
| 3 | tablespoons freshly-squeezed lime juice |
| 1 | tablespoon kosher salt |
| 1 | tablespoon sugar |
| | tortilla chips |

In a medium bowl, combine all ingredients. Place in refrigerator for flavor infusion, at least 1 hour. Serve with tortilla chips, if desired.

Mary grows several flavorful varieties of zucchini, including Spineless Beauty, Cash Flow, and a glossy yellow hybrid called Golden Dawn. The secret to Basi Italia's justifiably famous antipasto is a quick and ever-so-slight sauté of young, tender zucchinis, maintaining freshness and firmness as it mingles with toasted almonds and gurgling olive oil. For the finishing touch, it's draped with paper-thin sheets of pecorino romano cheese, shaved with a vegetable peeler. Add more nuts if you desire a higher almond-to-zucchini ratio.

# Zucchini Pronto

*makes 2 servings*

## SIDE DISH

| | |
|---|---|
| 3 | tablespoons extra virgin olive oil |
| 2 | tablespoons raw slivered almonds |
| 1 | medium (or 2 small zucchinis), unpeeled, cut into 1 1/2" matchsticks |
| | juice of 1/2 lemon |
| 1 | tablespoon chopped fresh flat-leaf parsley |
| | salt |
| | black pepper, freshly-cracked |
| 6–8 | paper-thin sheets pecorino romano cheese |

1. Heat the oil on high in a large skillet. When it is hot but not smoking, add the almonds to the pan. Cook them, while stirring, until the almonds are golden brown, about 1 or 2 minutes.

2. Add the zucchini to the pan, tossing it with the oil and almonds until it just begins to glisten, about 1 minute. Keep the pan moving, ensuring the zucchini is completely coated in the olive oil and there is good almond distribution.

3. Remove from the heat. Add the parsley and lemon juice, season with salt and pepper to taste, and toss to coat.

4. To serve, quickly remove from the pan and divide between 2 warmed plates; layer the cheese sheets over the top to cover. Allow cheese to melt with the heat of the zucchini for 1 minute before serving.

# DAVIDSON PRODUCE AND CATTLE FARM

**"Our mission is** to treat the land and animals God created for us with dignity and respect," says Wendy Davidson, who, along with husband Rodney, raises cattle, pigs, and chickens on a small farm just north of Newark. "This is land we deeply care about, where we live and raise our children," she says. "The food we bring to the Market is the same food we serve our family."

The meats have their own taste, the taste of the farm. From the time they are weaned from their mother's milk, cattle are rotationally grazed among different fields giving livestock access to pasture at the peak of nutrition and letting the animals spread manure evenly over the entire pasture, a valuable asset to the restoration of fertility to the soil. During the winter months they feed on good-quality hay from a neighboring hayfield, without grain supplementation and without steroids or antibiotics. For the Davidsons, feeding on pasture is an important part of ensuring that the animals have comfortable, healthy living conditions.

"You've got to have a personal connection with animals in order to be able to successfully raise them," says Wendy. "It's interesting to come to our house. We'll often have cows grazing in our front yard, sometimes looking in the windows."

Beef is processed in a spotless, stainless steel cutting room and dry-aged for a minimum of fourteen days. It comes back to the Davidsons cut, weighed, sealed in airtight packages and frozen – ready for sale at the Market.

Just as they seemed lost in history, small family farms are bouncing back, re-invigorating the local food system. "It's a lot of work, but it's a simpler, slower life," explains Wendy. "We take care of the animals, we watch them grow, and we know we're doing something good – we're helping to feed people, and that's important."

# Coq au Vin with Saffron

*makes 6 servings*

Davidson Farm's hybrid "Cornish Rock" chickens have large, meaty thighs and legs, perfect birds for simmering in the rustic Burgundian dish, as interpreted by Chef Matthew Litzinger of L'Antibes. "Serve with potatoes or over egg noodles," implores the chef, "and peas are very good alongside." Cook with a wine that you like to drink, so you'll have something to sip while preparing the dish.

## MAIN DISH

| | |
|---|---|
| 1/2 | pound bacon slices |
| 3 | pounds chicken thighs and legs, excess fat trimmed, skin on |
| 20 | pearl onions, peeled (or 1 large yellow onion, sliced) |
| 6 | garlic cloves, peeled |
| | salt |
| | black pepper, freshly-cracked |
| 2 | cups organic chicken stock |
| 2 | cups Firelands Pinot Noir or other red wine |
| 1 | teaspoon saffron, dissolved in a few tablespoons of water |
| 2 | bay leaves |
| 6 | sprigs fresh thyme |
| 6 | sprigs of fresh parsley |
| 1/2 | pound button mushrooms, trimmed and roughly chopped |
| 2 | tablespoons butter |
| | chopped fresh parsley, for garnish |

1. Brown bacon on medium high heat in a dutch oven big enough to hold the chicken, about 10 minutes. Remove the cooked bacon, set aside. Keep the bacon fat in the pan. Lightly, flour the chicken and shake off any excess. Working in batches if necessary, add onions and chicken, skin side down. Brown the chicken well, on all sides, about 10 minutes. Halfway through the browning, add the garlic and season the chicken with salt and pepper to taste.

2. Spoon off any excess fat. Add the chicken stock, wine, saffron, and herbs. Add back the bacon. Lower heat to a simmer. Cover and cook for 20 minutes, or until chicken is tender and cooked through. Remove chicken and onions to a separate platter. Remove the herbs and bay leaves.

3. Add mushrooms to the remaining liquid and turn the heat to high. Boil quickly and reduce the liquid by three fourths until it becomes thick and saucy. Lower the heat, stir in the butter. Return the chicken and onions to the pan to reheat and coat with sauce. Adjust seasonings.

4. Remove chicken and place in a casserole dish for serving. Pour the sauce over and around the chicken, and scatter the chopped parsley over the top. Serve family-style around the table.

Flank steak is a lean, flavorful cut of beef, although somewhat tough. For his preparation, Chef Bill Glover of Sage American Bistro, tenderizes the steak in a savory marinade and cooks it quickly at high heat. His recipe calls for grilling the steak, but if you don't have a grill, you can prepare the steak on a large cast iron frying pan as well. As accompaniment, the chef suggests serving a side of pommes frites and a raw kale salad garnished with the remaining cucumber aioli.

# Grilled Flank Steak
## with Cucumber Aioli Marinade

*makes 4–6 servings*

**THE MARINADE**

| | |
|---|---|
| 1 | seedless cucumber, chopped |
| 1 | jalapeño pepper, chopped (seeds removed, if desired) |
| 2 | garlic clove |
| 1/2 | cup chopped parsley |
| 1 | egg yolk |
| 1 | cup vegetable oil |
| 2 | teaspoons salt |
| 1 | tablespoon black pepper, freshly-cracked |
| 1 | flank steak (1 1/2 to 2 pounds) |

**1.** Combine the cucumber, jalapeno, parsley, garlic in a blender, and puree until smooth. Add the egg yolk and pulse to mix. On low, slowly stream in the oil to form an emulsion.

**2.** Score the surface of the steak with ¼" deep knife cuts, about an inch apart, across the grain of the meat. Place the steak in a zip-top bag with half of the marinade. Refrigerate overnight.

## THE FRITES

| | |
|---|---|
| 3 | large Yukon Gold potatoes |
| | oil, for frying |
| | chopped fresh herbs |
| | (parsley, tarragon, rosemary) |
| | salt and pepper, to taste |

1. Cut the potatoes into long wedges and cover with water. In a medium pot, put enough cold water to cover the potatoes by at least an inch. Season the water with salt and add the potatoes to the pot, cook over medium heat until the potatoes are very soft, never boiling the water. Carefully remove the potatoes and drain on a towel. Place the potatoes on a plate and store in the freezer for an hour.

2. Preheat the grill with high, direct heat. Remove the steak from marinade and place on the hot grill, 4 minutes on each side, flipping every minute (best cooked to medium-rare). Rest the steak on a cutting board for 5 minutes after cooking.

3. Slice the steak into strips running against the grain of the meat, and divide among warmed dinner plates. Serve with the frites. butter over the popcorn and sprinkle with the salt-pepper-cumin mix to taste.

4. To finish the fries, heat 3 inches of oil in a medium pot to 325° F. Making sure not to overcrowd, carefully add the potatoes to the oil and fry until golden. Season the frites with fresh herbs, salt and pepper.

## FOR THE DISH

1. Preheat the grill with high, direct heat. Remove the steak from marinade and place on the hot grill, 4 minutes on each side, flipping every minute (best cooked to medium-rare). Rest the steak on a cutting board for 5 minutes after cooking.

2. Slice the steak into strips running against the grain of the meat, and divide among warmed dinner plates. Serve with the frites.

The exact origin of Carbonara is unknown, which leaves room for endless variations and opinions. Some say it was created by Italian women hoping to lure American soldiers at the end of World War II, whipping up an American breakfast into pasta. Whatever the real origin, the dish continues to inspire an almost religious reverence. Spaghetti is the choice of traditionalists like Chef Carly Sifritt of the Jury Room, but any pasta that holds the sauce will work as well.

# Pasta Carbonara
# with Davidson Farm Bacon

*makes 4 servings*

## MAIN DISH

| | |
|---|---|
| 2 | tablespoons olive oil |
| 1/2 | pound thick-cut bacon, diced |
| 2 | garlic cloves, peeled and minced |
| 1 | white onion, diced |
| 1 | small zucchini, diced |
| 1/4 | cup diced sun-dried tomatoes |
| 1/2 | cup chopped arugula |
| 2 | whole eggs and 2 egg yolks, room temperature |
| 1 | cup grated parmesan cheese |
| | salt |
| | black pepper, freshly-cracked |
| 1 | pound fresh spaghetti |
| 1 | handful fresh parsley, chopped, for garnish |

1. Put a large pot of salted water on the stove over high heat and bring to boil.

2. Heat 1 tablespoon of the oil in a large skillet over medium heat, add the bacon, and sauté until the fat just renders, on the edge of crispness. Remove from heat and transfer to a large bowl. Add another tablespoon of olive oil to the pan, and toss in garlic, onion, zucchini, tomatoes, and arugula. Cook over medium heat until vegetables are tender. Remove from the heat and combine with the bacon.

3. In a mixing bowl, whisk together the eggs, yolks and half the parmesan. Season with salt and pepper to taste.

4. Add pasta to the boiling water and boil until al dente. Drain pasta and add to the bowl of bacon and vegetables. Stir in egg mixture, adding a bit of reserved pasta water if needed for creaminess.

5. To serve, mound into warmed serving bowls and garnish with chopped parsley. Pass remaining parmesan around the table.

# FOLCK
## FAMILY FARM

**They're a feast for the senses,** deliciously sweet, fragrant and colorful, and the arrival of local strawberries at the Market is one of the first signs of summer. Cindy and Robert Folck have earned a reputation for growing some of the best strawberries in the state.

"I didn't choose farming, farming chose me," explains Cindy. "I grew up on a beef cattle farm in a state north of here whose name we don't mention in Ohio. Here in Mechanicsburg, we are in an area where no one else was growing strawberries or brambles. My husband and I saw a need, decided to try it out, and it's worked well for us."

To accommodate demand at the Market, growing multiple varieties of strawberries, each with its own unique flavor profile, makes it possible to extend the local season. A sweet and spicy scent announces the arrival of Earliglow, small in size but bursting with flavor and intoxicating fragrance. Honeoye, developed at Cornell, ripen in mid-season with medium-large, firm, dark red berries. An old favorite, Jewel is a "trophy berry," productive late variety, large, firm, shiny, and delightfully sweet.

Fully-red, fully-ripe berries are hand-picked early in the morning of Market day and offered for sale within hours. "When we hear folks say, 'These are the best strawberries I ever had' or 'This is what strawberries used to taste like,' it makes our day. It's great to have that connection with people who enjoy something you work so hard to produce."

The Folck family also invites the public to their farm where "you pick-em." "We see the smiling faces of the kids when they're out there filling their buckets and the old-timers remembering when they used to do it and still can," she explains. "It's the fun part of growing strawberries."

Brunches can offer a wonderful, relaxed environment. Invite friends over for a summer gathering on the porch or patio and serve this healthy and flavorful housemade granola from Chef John Skaggs of the Heirloom Café. It's pretty enough for guests, and takes advantage of great-tasting, ripened-on-the-plant strawberries. Serve as individual parfaits or as a buffet item in a large trifle bowl.

# "Summer Brunch" Granola
## with Local Strawberries
## and Maple Whipped Cream

*makes 4 servings*

## GRANOLA

| | |
|---|---|
| 4 | cups rolled oats |
| 2 | tablespoons oat or spelt bran |
| 1 | teaspoon cinnamon |
| 1 | teaspoon kosher or sea salt |
| 2 | tablespoons brown sugar |
| 2 | tablespoons soybean or other vegetable oil |
| 1/2 | cup maple syrup |
| 1 | teaspoon vanilla extract |
| 2/3 | cup raw hazelnuts |
| 2/3 | cup dried blueberries |
| 2 | cups fresh strawberries, hulled and sliced maple whipped cream* |

* In a chilled mixing bowl, beat ½ cup of cold whipping cream until soft peaks form; add 2 tablespoons maple syrup and beat until firm. Makes about 1 cup of whipped cream.

1. Preheat oven to 250° F. In a large mixing bowl with a wooden spoon, mix together rolled oats, oat bran, cinnamon and salt. In a separate bowl, whisk together brown sugar, oil, honey and vanilla.

2. Pour the wet mix into the dry mix and stir to combine with a wooden spoon. Scrape the ingredients onto a sheet tray (at least 9" x 12"), making an even layer. Place sheet tray into pre-heated oven and bake for 15 minutes. Remove from oven and re-mix in bowl. Scrape the ingredients back onto the same sheet tray and bake for 15 minutes.

3. Remove from oven and re-mix with chopped hazelnuts and dried blueberries in bowl. Scrape the ingredients back onto the same sheet tray and bake for 15 minutes.

4. Remove from oven and scrape hot granola into a clean bowl to cool.

5. To serve, divide into 4 parfait glasses. Top each with strawberries and a dollop of the whipped cream.

# Frozen Tessora Soufflé
## with Local Raspberry Coulis

*makes 6 servings*

Italian for "treasure," Tessora is a creamy, lemon-flavored digestif, made in nearby New Albany from a 200-year-old family recipe. While the drink is traditionally a final, stand-alone bookend to a meal, Chef Richard Blondin of The Refectory kills two birds with one stone. His revelatory Tessora-based dessert satisfies the post-dinner sweet tooth and settles the stomach at the same time. A purée of Folck Family Farm raspberries provides an inspired finishing touch. Indulge to your heart's content.

### THE RASPBERRY COULIS

| | |
|---|---|
| 3/4 | cup sugar |
| 1 1/2 | pints fresh raspberries |

Combine sugar, berries, and ½ cup water in a saucepan. Bring to a boil over medium-high heat. Reduce heat to medium low; cook until sugar is dissolved, 6 to 8 minutes. Remove from heat; cool completely. Place mixture in a blender and purée until smooth. Set aside.

### THE SOUFFLÉ

| | |
|---|---|
| 1 1/2 | cups heavy cream |
| 7 | large egg yolks |
| 1 | cup sugar |
| 3 | ounces water |
| 2 1/2 | ounces Tessora Crema al Limone Liqueur |

1. Whip heavy cream until soft peaks form and set aside. Whip egg yolks until fluffy while sugar mixture is boiling. In sauce pot, boil sugar and water until soft ball state (244° F). Slowly pour hot syrup into whipped egg yolks. Continue beating until mix is cool and fluffy. Drizzle the liqueur into the sugar/egg mix. Fold mixture into the whipped cream.

2. Make collars from aluminum foil strips and wrap around 6 small ramekins so that the upper edges are 1" above the tops. Oil and sugar-coat the insides of the collars. Fill piping bag with mix just shy of rim (⅛"). Swirl a skewer to make even layers. Place in freezer overnight.

3. To serve, remove the foil collars from the dishes and place each on a dessert plate. Garnish each portion with the raspberry coulis and serve cold.

**He is single-handedly responsible** for creating a multitude of local honey snobs. High school science teacher turned master beekeeper, Isaac Barnes provides home to about 200 colonies of bees on the family farm in Williamsport and harvests between sixty and one hundred pounds of "locally grown" honey each year. Once you've tasted the golden nectar, it's like discovering a fine wine.

Unlike large-scale producers who fine and filter their honey for clarity and cook it to prevent crystallization, Isaac's raw honey is crafted under the artisan's watchful eye, processed with minimum heat and gently strained through a mesh screen to retain pollen and healthful enzymes.

Isaac works diligently to isolate the produce of his bees, obtaining honeys that reflect carefully-chosen fields, orchards, and wide meadows of wildflowers in Pickaway County – not only the flavor, color, and perfume of each individual floral source, but the characteristics of each year's growing season. Marketgoers have come to appreciate the subtle taste differences.

Spring Harvest is a light, mild, and delicate honey, sourced primarily from the blossoms of black locust and Russian olive trees in Deer Creek Valley. Summer Harvest is sprightly sweet with caramel and fruit flavors, mostly from clover, Canadian thistle, and wild blackberries. Fall Harvest is rich, robust, and intensely flavorful (with subtle notes of butterscotch and mint), a deep amber honey collected from goldenrod and aster flowers. These extraordinary honeys can be used as sweeteners in coffee or tea, in marinades for game, married to a plate of cheeses, or in the fixings of a charming dessert.

Isaac's wife Jayne uses the abundance of honey and beeswax to produce bars of sweet-smelling farmstead soaps and drip-free, long-burning candles. "Honey provides us a sustainable living," she says, "and it's something that benefits others as well."

# Honeyrun FARM

# "Fall Harvest"
## HONEY-ROASTED ROOT VEGETABLES

*makes 4-6 servings*

Derived from the nectar of flowers, honey has been used to describe everything from sweetness to sensuality, and even as a metaphor for goodness. Choose the vegetables for this dish according to preference and availability. The robust nectar adds sweetness and sheen; walnuts and thyme sprigs roast along with the vegetables for additional fall flavor.

### SIDE DISH

| | |
|---|---|
| 2 | medium sweet potatoes, peeled, halved, and cut into 1/2"pieces |
| 4 | medium carrots, cut into 1/2" pieces |
| 2 | medium parsnips, peeled and cut into 1/2" pieces |
| 1/2 | cup walnut halves |
| 1/4 | cup Honeyrun Farm "Fall Harvest" honey |
| 2 | tablespoons olive oil |
| | salt |
| | black pepper, freshly-cracked |
| 3-5 | sprigs thyme |

1. Preheat oven to 375° F. In a 3-quart baking dish, toss together sweet potatoes, carrots, parsnips, and walnuts with honey and oil. Season with salt and pepper to taste. Top with thyme sprigs and roast until vegetables are browned at edges and tender when pierced with a knife, about 1 hour.

2. To serve, transfer to a warmed bowl and pass family-style around the table.

# The Hibiscus Bee's Knees

*makes 1 drink*

The attraction of bees to the nectar of hibiscus flowers inspires drinksmith Logan Demmy of Mouton in his interpretation of the post-Prohibition "Bee's Knees" cocktail. Logan adds a floral flavor profile to Watershed vodka with hibiscus powder (from North Market Spices), blends with citrus and honey (from Honeyrun Farm), and teases the palate with a hint of cherries from maraschino liqueur.

## COCKTAIL

| | |
|---|---|
| 2 | ounces infused vodka * |
| 1/2 | ounce lemon juice, freshly-squeezed |
| 1/2 | ounce honey syrup ** |
| 1/4 | ounce Luxardo Maraschino liquor |
| | lemon wheel, thinly-sliced, for garnish |

Combine the vodka, lemon juice, honey syrup, and liqueur with ice in a shaker. Shake vigorously and strain into a pre-chilled cocktail coupe. Float the lemon wheel on the surface of the drink and serve.

*Add 2 tablespoons hibiscus powder to a 1-liter bottle of Watershed vodka. Infuse for 24 hours, then strain through a coffee filter and re-bottle.*

**Combine equal parts honey and water in a saucepan. Heat until thoroughly mixed. Cool and refrigerate. The syrup will be good for up to six months.*

"She sent him Lavender, owning her love," wrote William Shakespeare. Lavender's seductive floral and spicy aroma and notes of mint and lemon combine with rich flavors of local honey in yummy cupcakes, handcrafted by Lara Ranallo of the Surly Girl Saloon. Although the wooly-looking leaves are fragrant and edible, the pretty purple flowers and buds are the best for cooking. Frost each cupcake, then garnish with a single fresh blossom on top.

# Honey and Lavender Cupcakes
## with Honey-Vanilla Buttercream Frosting

*makes 3 dozen cupcakes*

### THE CUPCAKES

| | |
|---|---|
| 5 | cups all-purpose flour |
| 2 | teaspoons salt |
| 2 | teaspoons baking soda |
| 8 | ounces fresh lavender |
| 2 1/2 | cups sugar |
| 3 | cups vegetable oil |
| 2 | cups buttermilk |
| 2 | teaspoons cider vinegar |
| 1 | tablespoon vanilla extract |
| 4 | eggs at room temperature |
| 3/4 | cup Honeyrun Farm honey |
| | buttercream frosting (from below) |
| | lavender blossoms, for garnish |

### THE FROSTING

| | |
|---|---|
| 1 | pound butter, softened |
| | seeds of 2 vanilla beans |
| 1/4 | cup Honeyrun Farm honey |
| 2 | tablespoons fresh lavender, pulsed in a food processor |
| 1 | pound powdered sugar |

In the bowl of a mixer fitted with a paddle attachment, combine the butter with the vanilla bean seeds. Add the honey and lavender and mix at medium speed until combined. Gradually add the powdered sugar until ingredients are thoroughly combined and smooth and creamy. (For a lavender tint, add a few drops of red and blue food coloring.)

1. Preheat the oven to 350° F. In a large mixing bowl, combine the flour, salt and baking soda by hand. Set aside.

2. Pulse the lavender in food processor. Transfer to a mixing bowl and combine with the sugar. Mix the lavender sugar with the flour mixture.

3. In a mixer, combine the vegetable oil, buttermilk, cider vinegar, vanilla extract, eggs and honey. Slowly add in the dry ingredients until thoroughly combined. Portion batter by filling cupcake liners 3/4 full and bake for 20 to 22 minutes or until a toothpick inserted in the center of a cupcake comes out clean.

4. Remove from oven and place on a wire rack to cool. Once the cupcakes have completely cooled, frost with icing and garnish each with a lavender blossom. The cupcakes are best eaten the same day they are made, but they can be covered and stored for a few days.

# Crispy Brussels Sprouts
## with Honey, Lemon, Chili, and Almonds

*makes 4 servings*

"Honey adds a subtle but perceptible depth to everything it encounters," says Chef Andrew Bell of Latitude 41. Crispy on the outside and tender on the inside, when you glaze them with local honey and lemon, brussels sprouts are transformed. Depending on the size of the baby cabbages, cut into halves or quarters.

### SIDE DISH

|       |                                                                      |
|-------|----------------------------------------------------------------------|
|       | canola oil, for deep-frying                                          |
| 1/4   | cup honey                                                            |
| 2     | lemons, juiced and strained                                         |
| 1     | large handful brussels sprouts, trimmed and halved or quartered     |
| 1/2   | teaspoon crushed red chili flakes (If you are a fan of heat, be generous.) |
| 1/3   | cup toasted and coarsely-chopped almonds                            |

1. Pour enough oil into a medium pot so that the oil comes 3 inches up the sides. Heat the oil to 350° F. While the oil is heating, whisk together the honey and lemon juice until emulsified. Set aside.

2. Working in batches, deep-fry the brussels sprouts. (Be aware that as soon as you drop the sprouts into the liquid, they will release and pop oil, so please be careful). As soon as the sprouts turn to a dark green/golden brown and edges begin to curl, remove from the pot and drain on paper towels to remove excess oil.

3. Place into a serving bowl, add the chili flakes and honey-lemon glaze. Toss to coat. Sprinkle with the almonds and pass family-style around the table.

**Down along the western bend of the Ohio River, generations of Adams County's farmers grew tobacco as their primary cash crop. As demand dwindled, resourceful farmers have found that the fertile soils are also suited for growing vegetables.**

He studied agriculture in college, but after graduating, Robert Klouman became a teacher. Then in 1997, on a 47-acre former tobacco farm in Blue Creek, he decided to roll up his sleeves and put his degree to work.

"Running a family farm," says Robert, "has become close to impossible without a working spouse and a produce niche." He and Kim (the "K" of "K and R") grow many things others aren't bringing to the Market, allowing them to focus on crops that do well in their soil and which they especially enjoy growing.

One oddity is "Malabar" or Indian spinach with fleshy, thick leaves and flavor notes of citrus and pepper. "It doesn't wilt as fast as regular spinach," says Robert, and it holds up better in soups and stir-fries." Another distinctive crop is squash blossoms, the dainty, edible flowers of summer squashes with tiny hints of mushroom and squash flavors. "They are far too fragile for most supermarkets to handle," he explains, "so folks look for them at the Market."

"We have a great place to grow Asian eggplants," says Robert, "and we have ten different varieties." "Asian Bride" is a pretty bi-colored fruit shaped like long fingers; "Orient Express" is a slender, glossy deep purple fruit. Both have more delicate flavor than American eggplants. "They are wonderful on the grill," he explains to Market shoppers. "The skin holds the eggplant together and protects the flesh from the flame."

He loves growing them, he loves sharing them, and he loves talking about them.

# K AND R GARDEN FRESH PRODUCE

Raw Malabar spinach has very fleshy, thick leaves that are juicy and crisp with tastes of citrus and pepper. It gets treated to a quick sauté in partnership with savory garlic for the perfect side dish, and a pinch or two of nutmeg provides a subtle background lift.

# Wilted Malabar Spinach
## "Scented with Garlic"

*makes 4 servings*

### SIDE DISH

| | |
|---|---|
| 16 | ounces fresh malabar spinach |
| 1/4 | cup extra-virgin olive oil |
| 3 | cloves garlic, peeled and sliced paper-thin |
| 2 | pinches of ground nutmeg or fresh grated nutmeg |
| | sea salt |
| | black pepper, freshly-cracked |

**1.** Pick spinach free of large stems, wash well and drain in colander to allow water to drip off.

**2.** Heat a large skillet over moderate heat and add the olive oil. Add spinach in bunches, wilting and turning leaves in the pan. Halfway through, toss in the garlic and continue to add the remaining spinach. Cook the spinach until just wilted, about 5 minutes. Season with nutmeg, salt and pepper to taste.

**3.** Serve family-style from a warmed bowl or divide among 4 side dishes.

# Grilled "Asian Bride" Eggplants
## WITH SWEET RED PEPPERS

*makes 4 servings*

Small Asian eggplants have thinner skins, a more delicate flavor, and not as many of the seeds that tend to make eggplants bitter. Pretty, finger-shaped "Asian Brides" mature to a blush over white bi-color with creamy flesh. Grilling adds a smoky note to this aromatic, miso-glazed dish. To complete the theme, serve with sake in ochoko cups, warmed to about 100° F.

### SIDE DISH

| | |
|---|---|
| 1/2 | cup white miso paste |
| 1/4 | cup sake (rice wine) |
| 2 | tablespoons sugar |
| 6 | Asian Bride or other Japanese eggplants, halved lengthwise |
| 2 | sweet red peppers, cut into wedges, stems and seeds removed |
| 1/4 | cup canola oil |
| | salt |
| | black pepper, freshly-cracked |
| | chopped basil, for garnish |
| 2 | cups cooked rice |

**1.** Whisk together the miso, sake, sugar and 2 table-spoons water until smooth. Brush the eggplant and peppers with the oil and season with salt and pepper.

**2.** On a pre-heated grill, brush the peppers with the glaze and grill, turning with tongs every 2 minutes, until the surface begins to char. Remove the blistered peppers from the grill and set aside.

**3.** Brush the eggplant with the glaze and place on the grill, about 4 minutes. Flip over, brush with more of the glaze and continue grilling for a few more minutes, until the eggplant is caramelized. Remove from the grill.

**4.** To serve, divide eggplant halves and pepper wedges onto each of 4 warmed dishes, and sprinkle with the chopped basil. Pass a bowl of cooked rice family-style around the table.

# LUCKY CAT bakery and farm

**The best compliment you'll ever hear** from an Italian baker is, "He's as good as bread!" This saying could very well apply to Andrew Semler and his vocation. What's so good about Lucky Cat is what it is not. It's not your average bakery, and for that matter, it's not your average farm.

His passion for food began as a schoolboy. Andrew began formal training at the Natural Gourmet Institute in New York, where he studied the effect of food on health and well-being. In 2000, following an apprenticeship in a Japanese restaurant kitchen, he ran a seasonal sushi bar on Cape Cod before becoming victim to the "seven year itch." In his words, "I had achieved everything I had strived to do, and I decided it was time to move on."

In 2007, after re-connecting with his high school sweetheart and falling in love, he followed her out to Columbus. Still interested in working with food, he took a leap and purchased a seven-acre farm in rural Pataskala, intent on trying his hand at growing vegetables (even though he had never so much as attempted a garden). He began selling on a small scale at the Granville Farmers Market, and at the end of the first season he bought a copy of Peter Reinhart's *The Bread Baker's Apprentice* and a new oven. The following year he expanded his offerings with rustic ciabatta and baguettes. "My customers were enthusiastic, so I knew I was on to something," he says, as baking began to take over his life.

It's a good thing he set up his bakery in the farmhouse, as he often works 15 straight hours to hand-form and bake hundreds of his signature items in time for Saturday at the North Market. "Among our ten artisan breads, folks seem to really like our focaccia," says Andrew. "It's made with virgin olive oil and topped with sea salt, and it's got nice big open holes – so pillowy, soft and fluffy you could sleep on it!"

According to James Beard, "Too few people understand a really good sandwich." The modern version of the grilled cheese sandwich originated in the 1920s when inexpensive sliced bread and American cheese became easily available. But today there's no reason to just stick to boring fromage and ordinary bread. Granville Inn's Chad Lavely unites cheeses (think local) and chewy, artisanal bread from the Lucky Cat ovens in a yin-yang sort of way. It's a sophisticated interpretation of the familiar icon.

# Granville Inn's
# TOASTED CHEESE

*makes 4 servings*

## SANDWICH

| | |
|---|---|
| 1 | loaf Lucky Cat French bread |
| 2 | ounces cream cheese, softened |
| 1 | tablespoon Dijon mustard |
| 2 | teaspoons prepared horseradish |
| 4 | slices (2 ounces) Mayfield Road Creamery Smoked Gouda |
| 4 | slices (2 ounces) Minerva Dairy Cheddar Cheese |
| 1 | stick butter, melted |

1. Combine softened cream cheese, Dijon mustard, and horseradish until well mixed, set aside. Remove the heel from the loaf of bread, then slice into 8 slices, about ½-¾" thick.

2. Preheat pan of choice over medium heat, generously brush both sides of the bread with the melted butter, then cook the slices on the first side until toasty and golden. Repeat until you have all the slices cooked on one side

3. Move the slices to your work surface toasted side up. Spread 1 tablespoon of the reserved cream cheese mixture on the toasted side of each slice of bread. Top each slice with the gouda followed by the cheddar, lastly placing another slice of bread over the cheese. Be certain to place the toasted side in.

4. Cook sandwiches until both sides are golden and toasty, and the cheese is melted.

NOTE *You can hold the sandwiches in a warm oven while you finish cooking. Place them on a wire rack over a sheet pan to allow air to move around them to avoid a soggy bottom. If the sandwiches brown before the cheese melts, you can also finish them in the oven for a few minutes.*

# Rillettes de Canard

*makes 4 servings*

In farmhouse tradition, for the past few years Andrew has raised Muscovy ducks for personal consumption. "I normally part them out and save the breasts for pan frying or grilling," he explains, "and confit the legs for rillettes." The earthy concoction is a specialty of the French Loire Valley and nearby regions, traditionally made by pounding confit into a tender, succulent, spread. "I spread it on my own sourdough bread along with cornichons, capers, and thinly-sliced shallots," says Andrew. "Whole grain mustard is good too."

## THE CONFIT

| | |
|---|---|
| 1 | teaspoon black pepper, freshly-cracked |
| 1/2 | teaspoon dried thyme |
| 1 | bay leaf, crumbled |
| 4 | duck legs, not trimmed |

1. In a small bowl, combine salt, pepper, thyme and bay leaf, and season duck legs with the mixture. Cover the bowl tightly with plastic wrap, and refrigerate overnight.

2. Heat duck legs in a skillet over medium heat until fat starts to render, about 20 minutes. Transfer legs to an ovenproof baking dish, and cover with warm fat. Cook in oven 1½ to 2 hours, until duck is golden brown. Remove from the oven, cool to room temperature on a rack, and put in refrigerator, covered, until ready to use.

## THE RILLETTES

| | |
|---|---|
| 4 | confit of duck legs |
| 4 | tablespoons duck fat |
| 1 | garlic clove |
| | salt |
| | black pepper, freshly-cracked |

1. Pull meat off of duck legs and coarsely chop. Remove skin and discard bones (you can fry the skin until well crisped; coarsely chop and add to the rillettes at the end for extra flavor and texture).

2. In a mortar put a pinch of salt and the garlic. Pound with pestle until it becomes a smooth paste, then add a bit of the fat and meat; pound until smooth. Continue until you use half the meat and all the fat. Fold in the remainder of the meat until it is evenly distributed. Spoon into 4 ramekins and refrigerate until ready to serve.

3. Before serving, remove from fridge about 2 hours ahead, letting it get to room temperature (the fat melts a bit and more flavors come through). Serve with a chewy bread and a simple green salad.

# OINK MOO CLUCK FARM

**Listen carefully.** These are the sounds you'd expect to hear on a farm that raises beef, pork, and chicken.

It was their grandfather who began the family tradition in 1947, so you might say that Todd Neczeporenko and Tricia Woods have farming in their DNA. A native of Ukraine, grandpa Mykola arrived in Pierpont, Ohio, a small agricultural community not far from Lake Erie, where he began raising livestock. His son Tim expanded the enterprise with the purchase of a nearby meatpacking plant, and following in the footsteps of both his grandfather and father, the lure of the family business came calling to Todd. "As the third generation," he admits, "I learned most of what I know growing up right here on the farmstead."

"We control every stage of the process," explains Todd. "Our animals live their entire lives on the lush pasture grasses – they never see a feed lot where they might be crowded together with many animals. They are humanely processed and packed in our own butcher shop – and we sell directly to customers at the North Market as well as other markets around the state."

His herd ranges from 50 to 100 cattle, cross-bred varieties of Black Angus, and 100 to 200 Berkshire pigs, but Todd is less obsessed with specific breeds and more interested in good-quality genetics, and in his words, "feeding them according to the way they want to eat and without the aide of hormones or antibiotics." Breed does count, however, when it comes to his flock of 400 to 500 pasture-raised Cornish-Rock chickens, remarkable for their broad breasts and big thighs, or as he calls them, "plump, tender, and naturally delicious."

"Our customers want to know where their food comes from, how it's raised, who processed it, and who transported it," says Tricia, who manages sales at the Market. If she has her way, Columbus will always have access to the best her family has to offer.

When the Lazarus Department Store in downtown Columbus closed in August 2004, it marked the end of an era. Many longtime residents have fond memories of the Chintz Room, the store's fifth floor dining room, where women wore hats and white gloves and lunch was a social event. One favorite dish lives on in a nostalgic recipe adapted from *A Treasury of Favorite Recipes from Lazarus*: "The Chintz Room's Chicken Salad is probably the most requested recipe, and though it appears simple, it requires a particular flair. The pecans provide a unique character, but you might substitute or add raisins, walnuts, or dates."

# "Chintz Room" Chicken Salad with Toasted Pecans

*makes 4 servings*

### THE POACHED CHICKEN

**3 chicken breasts, boneless and skinless**

Cut chicken breasts into 2 to 3" pieces. Bring a 2-quart pot of well-salted water to a rolling boil. Add the chicken to the boiling water, turn off the heat and cover the pot. Hold chicken in the hot water for 15 minutes, then drain the water and cut the chicken pieces into smaller cubes for the salad. Place in the fridge to chill.

### THE SALAD

| | |
|---|---|
| 1 | **pound poached chicken (from above)** |
| 2 | **stalks celery, chopped** |
| 3/4 | **cup dressing (from right)** |
| 4 | **large leaves of iceberg lettuce** |
| 3/4 | **cup pecans, toasted and chopped** |

1. Mix chicken and celery together and gently stir in the dressing.

2. To serve, arrange on 4 chilled plates in individual lettuce cups. Sprinkle pecans over the top of each.

### THE DRESSING

| | |
|---|---|
| 1/4 | **cup cider vinegar** |
| 1/4 | **cup water** |
| 3 | **egg yolks** |
| 2 | **tablespoons sugar** |
| 1 | **teaspoon dry mustard** |
| 1 | **tablespoon all-purpose flour** |
| 1/8 | **teaspoon paprika** |
| 1 | **teaspoon sea salt** |
| 1/2 | **teaspoon pepper** |
| 2 | **tablespoons unsalted butter** |
| 1/2 | **cup sour cream** |

1. Pour the vinegar and water into a saucepan and bring to a boil. Put the egg yolks in a small mixing bowl and stir in the sugar, mustard, flour, paprika, salt, and pepper. Very slowly, pour the boiling vinegar/water into the egg yolk mixture, a small amount at a time, whisking well to make sure the vinegar/water mixture and the egg yolk mixture combine.

2. Pour the dressing back into the saucepan and cook, stirring constantly, over medium heat until it thickens. Remove from the heat and add the butter, whisking until it is melted and absorbed into the dressing. Whisk in the sour cream and cool completely. Cover and refrigerate.

The pork part that captures this chef's heart is, in fact, the last. "Pig tails make a great appetizer or main meat dish," says Magdiale Wolmark of Till Dynamic Fare, who serves pickled vegetables alongside. "The fat-to-meat content of tails is similar to pork belly and other succulent cuts." He cooks the tails twice, and the result is a crispy coating, smothered with a sauce made from Birney's Miracle Farm hot peppers. Look for pig tails that have a lot of meat around the upper part.

# Crispy Pig Tails
## with Market Hot Pepper Sauce

*makes 2 servings*

### THE HOT SAUCE

| | |
|---|---|
| 1/4 | pound mix of seasonal hot peppers (jalapeño, cayenne, habanero, etc.) |
| 1 | onion chopped |
| 3 | cloves garlic, minced |
| 1 | cup apple cider or rice wine vinegar |
| 2 | cups sugar |
| 1 | cup pig tail stock |
| 2 | cups preserved tomatoes |
| | salt |

Toss the peppers in just enough oil to coat them lightly and roast in 500° F. oven for 6 to 8 minutes or until the peppers begin to blister. Remove and chill. Take the stems off the peppers. Cook the onions in a little oil or bacon fat until they are soft and translucent. Add the garlic and cook an additional 30 seconds. Add the peppers and remaining ingredients and simmer for 30 minutes. Remove from heat, purée in a blender or food processor, and season with salt to taste.

## PIG TAIL FLOUR DREDGE/COATING

|     |                            |
| --- | -------------------------- |
|     | pig tails (from left)      |
| 2   | cups canola oil, for frying |
| I   | cup of flour               |
| 1/2 | teaspoon salt              |
| 1/2 | teaspoon paprika           |
| 1/2 | teaspoon onion powder      |
| 1/2 | teaspoon garlic powder     |
| 1/2 | teaspoon cumin             |
| 3   | eggs                       |
|     | hot pepper sauce (from far left) |

**1.** Preheat oven to 350° F. In a large cast iron skillet or stock pot, heat the oil to about 325° F. In a large mixing bowl, combine the flour and seasoning. In another large mixing bowl beat the eggs. Toss the tails in the flour, then the eggs, and then back into the flour. Fry the tails in the oil about 3 minutes and then turn and continue to fry for another 3 minute. Remove and place in the oven for 5 minutes.

**2.** In a wok or large skillet, heat 8 ounces of the hot sauce. When the tails are done, toss the tails 2 at a time in the wok with hot sauce, adding more sauce as needed so that the tails are thoroughly coated. Remove to warmed serving plates with a slotted spoon.

## THE PIG TAILS

|     |                               |
| --- | ----------------------------- |
| 1/4 | cup sugar                     |
| 1/8 | cup salt                      |
| 4   | medium size pig tails, shaved |
| I   | onion, chopped                |
| 2   | carrots, peeled and chopped   |
| 4   | garlic cloves, chopped        |
| 4   | stalks celery, chopped        |
| 2   | bay leaves                    |
| I   | cup red wine                  |
| 2   | cups meat or vegetable stock  |

**1.** Combine the sugar and salt in bowl and toss with the tails. Refrigerate for 1 to 3 days.

**2.** In a large stock pot or braiser, heat a small amount of oil or bacon fat over medium heat. Brown the tails on each side and remove from the pan. Add the vegetables and cook until tender, add the garlic and cook an additional 30 seconds.

**3.** Place the tails back in the pan and add the wine and bay leaf. Reduce by half. Add the stock, bring to a simmer, cover the pan and continue to cook over a very low flame for 2 hours. Remove the tails and chill. Strain the liquid and reserve.

**By late September, one particular table** at the Market is piled high with bulbous, ridged and long-necked squashes in shades of red, gold, orange, green, ivory and even blue. Some are solid colored, others striped. All are Cathy Persinger's passion.

# PERSINGER FARM

"Farming is the only life I know," says Cathy. "Growing up on my family's dairy farm, I was a member of both 4-H and the Future Farmers of America – and then I married a farmer!" For many years, she and husband Rock grew 120 acres of processing tomatoes for Heinz, but when the company failed to renew the yearly contract, Rock focused on field corn and soybeans and Cathy began raising market vegetables.

She has become a guardian of nature's diversity, growing a wide range of pumpkins and squashes. New England pie pumpkins are among crowd favorites, and peanut pumpkins are the ones that look like they've got peanuts growing all over them. No kidding. Her summer varieties include yellow squash, patty pans, and zucchini (best picked when they're about five to seven inches long). Winter squashes include acorn, butternut, hubbard, and delicata (or bohemian squash), whose flesh is some of the tastiest in the squash world. "Squash vines are incredibly tough and prolific," explains Cathy, "which is enough to make any farmer smile."

Her root vegetables include carrots, beets, turnips, potatoes, and sweet potatoes. "You would think the sweets would need a more sandy soil," she explains. "I put them in at the beginning of June, and they get gigantic – they're crazy about my soil for some strange reason."

"I love to eat, I love to cook, I love working outside," says Cathy, "and I love getting to share it all with so many wonderful folks at the Market."

When pumpkin season is in full swing, Chef Seifert's savory soup is the perfect first course for any meal. Try his recipe with Persinger Farm's peanut pumpkins, a light-colored heirloom winter squash first grown in the Bordeaux region of France and better known as *Brodé Galeux d'Eysine*, which means "embroidered with warts from Eysines." It tastes like a cross between pumpkin and sweet potato, tastier than many other cooking variety pumpkins. This soup can be made ahead and reheated when ready to serve.

# Chef Hubert Seifert's PUMPKIN SOUP

*makes 6 servings*

## SOUP

| | |
|---|---|
| 2 | pumpkins, about 4-pounds each |
| 1/4 | cup unsalted butter, cut into pieces |
| 1/4 | cup light brown sugar |
| 1/2 | tablespoon ground ginger |
| 1/2 | tablespoon ground mace |
| 1/4 | tablespoon ground nutmeg |
| | pinch of cayenne |
| | salt |
| 2 | cups heavy cream + extra for whipping |
| 2 | cups chicken stock |
| | pumpkin seeds, for garnish |

1. Preheat oven to 375° F. Cut the pumpkins in half, remove the seeds and fibers, and cut into wedges. Place the pieces, skin side down, in a shallow roasting pan. Cover with foil and bake until tender, about 1 ½ hours. When pumpkin pieces are cool enough to handle, remove the skins.

2. Place the pieces of pulp into a pot and toss with butter, sugar and spices. Add the chicken stock and heavy cream and bring to a simmer. Puree the soup in a food processor until smooth; do in small batches.

3. To serve, ladle into each of 6 warmed bowls. Add a dollop of whipped heavy cream to the surfaces and scatter toasted pumpkin seeds over each serving.

# "PUMPKIN PIE" Pancakes

*makes 4–6 servings*

These delicious pancakes embody many of the same ingredients as pumpkin pie, the quintessential autumn treat. Like pie, pancakes made from a fresh, local pumpkins taste so much better than canned purée from who knows where. The recipe yields six servings, if you're restrained.

## THE PUMPKIN PURÉE

| | |
|---|---|
| 1 | medium pie pumpkin (4-pounds) |

**1.** Preheat oven to 375° F. Spray a baking sheet with cooking spray. Using a small knife, remove the stem at the top and cut the pumpkin in half. Place halves face-side down onto baking sheet and bake until pumpkin is soft, about 45 minutes. Test for doneness by piercing with a fork. Turn over the pumpkin halves and let cool.

**2.** Gently scoop the soft pulp into a food processor or heavy-duty blender. Pulse until evenly puréed. Set aside.

## THE PANCAKES

| | |
|---|---|
| 1 3/4 | cups flour |
| 3 | tablespoons sugar |
| 1 | tablespoon ground cinnamon |
| 2 | teaspoons baking powder |
| 1 | teaspoon ground nutmeg |
| 1 | teaspoon ground ginger |
| 1 | teaspoon ground cloves |
| 1 | cup pumpkin purée (from below) |
| 1 | cup heavy cream |
| 1/2 | cup milk |
| 2 | eggs, beaten |
| 6 | tablespoons pumpkin seed or other vegetable oil butter and maple syrup, for serving |

**1.** In a large bowl, whisk together flour, sugar, cinnamon, baking powder, nutmeg, ginger, and cloves. Fold the pumpkin, cream, milk, and eggs into the dry ingredients. Whisk until smooth. Let batter rest for 10 to 15 minutes.

**2.** Heat 1 tablespoon of the oil in a large cast-iron skillet over medium-high heat. Pour batter into skillet to make the first batch of 3 to 5" diameter pancakes. Once bubbles begin to form on the edges, flip the pancake, cover pan and cook until golden and fluffy, about 1 to 2 minutes. Repeat with remaining oil and pancake batter.

**3.** To serve, stack pancakes on a warmed platter, and pass family style around the table with butter and maple syrup alongside.

# PROCTOR
## FARM

**For Rebekah Zimmerer, it's a dream fulfilled.** As a young girl growing up in Penobscot County, Maine, she imagined an idyllic life on a farm, and in her words, "I decided to figure it out as I go." After taking classes in international agriculture at Gordon College and studying the methods of traditional small scale farming, she became an apprentice at the historic Moraine Farm in Beverly, Massachusetts. "It was the beginning of a path that led me to Proctor Center," she explains, "and to the start-up of a unique farm project."

As part of an initiative regarding sustainable living, Thomas Breidenthal, bishop of the Episcopal Diocese of Southern Ohio, set aside a plot of land at the church's conference center and camp in London, Ohio to establish Proctor Farm. "I got the title of farm manager," says Rebekah. "It was kind of a leap, but it's been a really great experience, a growing and learning opportunity – it's a wonderful place to get your hands dirty."

More than fifty different vegetables are cultivated on two hilly acres of fertile soil, providing enough food to supply the conference center kitchen, make donations to local food pantries, and offer fresh-picked produce at the Market. "We just started growing Lunch Box peppers," she reports. "The colorful snack-size peppers are remarkably sweet and flavorful, turning red, yellow or orange as they mature. They grow 2 ½ inches wide and between 1 and 3 inches long, the perfect size for – you guessed it – lunch boxes."

According to Rebekah, "By connecting people with healthy food, the church demonstrates its stewardship commitment." She sees many parallels between serving a church and coordinating a farm project. "Both are about forming community, and both are about being connected to the community."

Inspired by the rustic *Sopa de Tortilla de Huevos*, Chef Kevin Eby of Betty's Fine Food & Spirits finishes this version with "pastured" eggs from Proctor Farm – from chickens that are allowed to do what chickens want to do naturally – wander around in the sun and open air. In the home kitchen, you can adjust the spices to get the heat and flavor your family likes best.

# Tortilla Soup with Fried Farm Eggs

*makes 4–6 servings*

### SOUP

| | |
|---|---|
| 2 | tablespoons vegetable oil |
| I | green bell pepper, finely-diced |
| I | cup yellow corn kernels |
| I | cup finely-diced tomatoes |
| I 1/2 | quarts chicken stock |
| I | tablespoon cayenne pepper |
| 1/2 | cup freshly-squeezed lime juice |
| 2 | tablespoons cumin |
| 2 | tablespoons garlic powder |
| 2 | tablespoons chili powder |
| 2 | boneless/skinless chicken breasts, grilled and diced |
| 1/4 | cup minced cilantro |
| 4 | eggs, lightly beaten |

**1.** Place a medium soup pot over medium-low heat, and add 1 tablespoon vegetable oil. Add bell pepper, corn, and tomatoes, and sauté, about 30 seconds.

**2.** Add chicken stock, lime juice, cayenne, cumin, garlic powder, and chili powder, and bring to a boil. Reduce heat to low, add grilled chicken and cilantro, and simmer for an additional 10 minutes.

**3.** While soup is cooking, place a small skillet over medium heat, and add 1 tablespoon oil. Add eggs and cook until firm, about 1 to 2 minutes. Remove omelet from pan and cut into 1"-wide slices.

**4.** To serve, ladle soup into warmed bowls; add omelet slices.

During three seasons of the year, the Proctor Farm pasture is alive with chicken hens, feeding on abundant grasses and grubs. Both breeds, the Barred Plymouth Rocks and Golden Comets, are efficient foragers and layers. "The brown eggs with deep yellow yolks are influenced by their diet and environment," explains Rebekah. To finish a salad inspired by the farm's pasture and herb garden, poached eggs are drizzled with good olive oil, grated with Pecorino, and seasoned from a few turns of the pepper mill.

# Parsley, Sage, Rosemary and Thyme Salad with Slow-Poached Eggs

*makes 4 servings*

## THE SALAD

| | |
|---|---|
| 6 | tablespoons chopped flat leaf parsley |
| 3 | tablespoons minced fresh sage |
| 3 | tablespoons minced fresh rosemary |
| 3 | tablespoons minced fresh thyme |
| 4 | bunches watercress, rinsed, dried and chopped |
| 1 1/2 | tablespoons balsamic vinegar |
| 1 1/2 | tablespoons olive oil + extra for drizzle |
| 4 | poached eggs (from left) |
| | grated pecorino cheese, as needed |
| | black pepper, freshly-cracked |

## POACHED EGGS

| | |
|---|---|
| 4 | eggs in shells |
| | water |
| | salt |

1. Add cold water with a pinch of salt to a heavy bottomed pot. Put a plate or wire rack in the bottom of the pan to prevent eggs from coming into direct contact with the heat source. Heat water to 140° F. and maintain temperature by leaving a thermometer attached to the side of the pot.

2. Add eggs and cook at this temperature for exactly 40 minutes, checking temperature regularly; add ice cubes if water gets too hot.

3. Remove eggs and gently crack shell, one at a time, into small individual saucers. Carefully pour off loosest part of white before serving.

1. In a medium-size bowl, toss together the parsley, sage, rosemary, thyme and watercress. Add the vinegar, olive oil, 1 teaspoon salt and pepper and mix well.

2. To serve, divide the salad among 4 chilled plates. Carefully slide a poached egg onto each salad, drizzle with olive oil, sprinkle with grated cheese, and season with pepper to taste.

# Quiver Full FARM

**"You can take the boy out of the farm,"** says Jim Barr, "but you can't take the farm out of the boy." He was raised on the family farm in Ashville, a sleepy village whose claim to fame is America's oldest working traffic light. In 1975, while working as a high school guidance counselor, Jim and his wife Karin bought the land adjacent to his boyhood home and began growing vegetables. By 2002, with five kids to put through college, they started selling the cream of their crop at the North Market. "I suppose I was always destined to be a farmer," says Jim.

Heirloom tomatoes are the pride of Quiver Full Farm, and although as many as fourteen different varieties are planted and painstakingly tended without the use of pesticides or herbicides, two in particular get most of the attention. The legendary Brandywine, whose lineage has been traced back through generations of Amish farmers, produces big, succulent fruit with sweet "tomatoey" essence offset by wonderful acidity. A century-old cultivar originating with Native Americans, Cherokee Purples have sweet yet complex flavor that he describes as slightly smoky or wine-like. "Marketgoers can't seem to get enough of these beauties," says Jim.

To accompany a ripe, juicy heirloom tomato, the grower suggests a bit of sea salt, a few leaves of basil, salami or other spiced meat, mozzarella cheese, and a drizzle of olive oil. It's the makings of a meal he enjoys practically every day from July until mid-October.

Quiver Full is a small farm with a big heart. "The scale of our venture isn't important to us at all," he explains. "We enjoy what we do together as a family and it's wonderful to have customers that appreciate it. We love the North Market because of the atmosphere and the encouragement to buy local."

A wise newspaperman by the name of Lewis Grizzard once wrote, "It's difficult to think anything but pleasant thoughts while eating a homegrown tomato." Jim Barr's gorgeous Brandywines partner with fresh local goat cheese in Chef Dan Varga's interpretation of the classic Florentine salad from the Explorers Club summer menu.

# "Brandywine" Panzanella with Local Goat Cheese *makes 4 servings*

## THE VINAIGRETTE

| | |
|---|---|
| 1 | small shallot, minced |
| 1 | clove of garlic, minced |
| 1 | tablespoon Dijon mustard |
| 1 | tablespoon chopped fresh thyme |
| 2 | tablespoons sugar |
| 1/2 | cup Valley Vineyards Cabernet Franc or other red wine |
| 1 | cup extra virgin olive oil |
| | salt |
| | black pepper, freshly-cracked |

Place all ingredients in a mason jar with a lid and shake vigorously. Season with salt and pepper to taste.

## THE SALAD

| | |
|---|---|
| 1 | loaf of day-old crusty Italian bread, cut into 1" cubes |
| 1 | English cucumber, cut into slices about 1/4" thick |
| 2 | Brandywine tomatoes, cored and cut into wedges or cubes |
| 1 | bunch fresh basil, picked from the stem, torn into little pieces |
| 1/2 | pound log Lucky Penny Farms or other fresh goat cheese, cut into 4 portions |
| 1/2 | cup julienned red onion |
| | red wine vinaigrette (from left) |

1. Place all ingredients except the cheese in a mixing bowl and toss with ½ cup of the red wine vinaigrette. Season with salt and pepper to taste. Let rest for 20 to 30 minutes before serving.

2. Divide salad among 4 chilled plates and place a portion of the goat cheese over each serving. Pass the extra vinaigrette alongside.

Fill your Market basket with the makings of the traditional French Provençal vegetable dish, but instead of sautéing the ingredients into a stew, put your mandolin to work and create a fanned, layered casserole – a more sophisticated showcase for individual flavor components of the fresh vegetables. The senses are connected in this dish – smell, sight, taste, and mouthfeel.

# Deconstructed Ratatouille

*makes 4 servings*

## MAIN DISH

| | |
|---|---|
| 2 | tablespoons olive oil |
| 1/2 | onion, finely chopped |
| 3 | garlic cloves, peeled and minced |
| 3 | heirloom tomatoes, peeled, seeded, and finely diced |
| 2 | tablespoons olive oil |
| 1 | small eggplant |
| 1 | zucchini |
| 1 | yellow squash |
| 1 | red bell pepper |
| | salt |
| | black pepper, freshly-cracked |

**1.** Heat the olive oil in a large skillet over medium heat. Sauté the onions, stirring occasionally, until soft and clear, about 5 minutes. Add the garlic and tomatoes and simmer the mixture, uncovered, for 10 minutes, stirring occasionally, until the sauce has thickened.

**2.** Pour tomato sauce into bottom of a casserole dish with 1 tablespoon of the olive oil. Trim the ends off the eggplant, zucchini and yellow squash. Carefully trim the ends off the red pepper and remove the core, leaving the edges intact.

**3.** On a mandolin, or with a very sharp knife, cut the eggplant, zucchini, yellow squash and red pepper into very thin slices, approximately 1/16" thick.

**4.** Down center of the casserole dish, arrange alternating slices of vegetables over the tomato sauce, overlapping so that 1/4 inch of each slice is exposed. Repeat until pan is filled. Drizzle the remaining tablespoon of olive oil over the vegetables and season with salt and pepper to taste.

**5.** Cover pan with foil and crimp edges to seal. Bake in a preheated oven at 375° F. until vegetables are fork tender and tomato sauce is bubbling up around them, about 40 to 45 minutes.

**6.** To serve, slice in quarters and with a spatula, and carefully lift onto 4 individual warmed plates. with salt and pepper to taste.

**Much depends on the fertile soil** of the Pickaway Plains, said to contain the richest land in all of Ohio. Here, over the past half century, the Rhoads family has planted, cultivated, and harvested fine fruits and vegetables on their Circleville farm.

Beginning in 1958, Robert and Lurose Rhoads, along with young son Brent, picked home-grown sweet corn and sold from a table at the end of their driveway. By 1961 they had installed a retail stand on State Route 56, where Robert and Lurose nurtured the business while Brent went away to college and the military.

Brent returned to the farm in 1972 along with his new wife Kathy, uncertain if there was enough income on the farm to support their future family. "We had to make some diversification of the operation," explains Kathy. "We added crops which lengthened the season, and expanded from a farm market into landscaping, a garden center, nursery, and off-site sales at the North Market beginning in 1979."

As the next generation of Rhoads became involved in the enterprise, Brett, who earned a degree in horticulture and crop science at Ohio State, inherited responsibility for the farm's 150-acre diverse mosaic of crops, taking special pride in strawberries, blackberries, sweet corn, melons, and brussels sprouts. Early-, mid-, and late-season varieties of the best-tasting sweet corn are hand-harvested and offered for sale, beginning just in time for Fourth of July picnics and barbeques.

"Is everybody happy?" That was the catchphrase of Circleville, Ohio's favorite son, Ted Lewis, the 1930s-era entertainer. Today, thanks to the Rhoads family, it's wonderful bounty from Circleville that brings good cheer to the Market.

# RHOADS FARM MARKET

# Noir 75

*makes 1 drink*

It was at New York's legendary Stork Club where the French 75 cocktail was, according to Lucius Beebe, author of the *Stork Club Bar Book*, "enshrined in the pharmacopoeia of alcohol artistry." Inspired by a genre of black-and-white films with hard-drinking heroes and femmes fatale, Rhoads Farm's dark, glossy blackberries heighten the shadows, while allowing local gin and sparkling wine to remain central characters.

## COCKTAIL

| | |
|---|---|
| 1 | ounce gin |
| 1/2 | ounce fresh-squeezed lemon juice |
| 3/4 | ounce blackberry syrup * |
| | chilled Champagne or other sparkling wine, to top up |

Place a tall flute in the freezer and chill at least 1 hour. Combine the gin, lemon juice, and blackberry syrup with ice in a shaker. Shake vigorously, then double strain into the pre-chilled flute. Top up with the wine. Serve without garnish.

*Combine 1½ cups of sugar, 1 cup of water, and 2 cups of fresh blackberries in a saucepan, and bring to a boil, stirring occasionally. When mixture comes to a boil, reduce heat and simmer for 5 to 7 minutes. Remove from heat and strain into a container. Store in refrigerator for up to 7 days.

"We use as many fresh, local vegetables as possible in our dishes," explains Chef Dan Varga of the Explorers Club, "and I like working with quinoa, a staple in Andean cultures but relatively obscure in the rest of the world." His recipe includes local sweet corn and other vegetables gathered at the Market. (The pickled mix will keep for up to a month in mason jars in the fridge).

# Hummus Quinoa Patty
## with Pickled Vegetables and Black Bean & Corn Relish

*makes 4–6 servings*

### THE PICKLED VEGETABLES

| | |
|---|---|
| 2 | large heads green cabbage, shredded |
| 4 | large carrots, peeled and cut into 1/2" moons |
| 4 | large cucumbers, sliced into wheels |
| 2 | large red peppers, cut into strips |
| 3 | pounds fresh Hungarian peppers, cut into rings |
| 2 | large yellow onion, cut into strips |
| 10 | cloves garlic |
| 8 | cups apple cider vinegar |
| 6 | cups water |
| 4 | cups sugar |
| 1 | cup salt |
| 3 | tablespoons pickle spice |

Bring the cider, water, sugar, salt, and pickle spice to a boil. Put all the veggies in a large container with a lid. Cover the veggies with the hot pickle brine and cover with a lid. Let stand in the cooler overnight.

## THE RELISH

| | |
|---|---|
| I | cup sweet chili sauce |
| I | cup cooked local black beans |
| I | cup fresh corn, cut off the cob, blanched |
| I | medium red pepper, diced |
| I | medium red onion, diced |
| 1/2 | cup apple cider vinegar |
| 1/2 | bunch cilantro, chopped |
| I | tablespoon chopped garlic |
| | salt |
| | black pepper, freshly-ground |

1. Place sweet chili sauce, vinegar, red pepper and onion in sauce pan and reduce on low flame by half. Add remainder of ingredients and season with salt and pepper to taste.

2. Chill for several hours.

## QUINOA PATTIES:

| | |
|---|---|
| I 1/2 | cups cooked quinoa |
| I 1/2 | cups hummus |
| 1/4 | cup chopped scallions |
| 1/4 | cup fresh corn, cut off the cob |
| 1/4 | cup chopped raw carrots |
| I | cup bread crumbs |
| I | tablespoon chopped garlic |
| I | tablespoon chopped fresh cayenne peppers |
| | salt |
| | black pepper, freshly-cracked |
| I | tablespoon safflower oil |
| | black bean and corn relish (from left) |
| | pickled vegetables (from far left) |

1. Knead together the quinoa, hummus, scallions, corn, carrots, bread crumbs, garlic, and peppers in a bowl until evenly combined. Adjust seasonings to taste. Divide into 4 or 6 equal portions and form into patties. Place patties in an oiled skillet over medium-high heat, and cook until browned on both sides.

2. When the patties are done, place each on a toasted bun, top each with the relish, and serve the pickles vegetables alongside.

"People are rediscovering the seasons," says Kathy Rhoads, "and nothing says 'summer' more than delicious sweet corn." A combination of sweet corn straight from the cob and fresh edamame (a specialty variety of soybean), this local succotash is bursting with flavors of summer, dancing together in the skillet, each vegetable maintaining its own delicate sweetness and individual flavor. Serve over brown rice to make it more of a meal rather than a side dish.

# Sweet Summer Corn and Edamame "Succotash"

*makes 4 servings*

### SIDE DISH

| | |
|---|---|
| 2 | cups fresh edamame, shells removed |
| 1 | tablespoon vegetable oil |
| 1 | red bell pepper, diced |
| 1/4 | cup red onion, diced |
| 2 | cloves garlic, sliced |
| 2 1/2 | cups fresh corn kernels (from 4 ears) |
| 3 | tablespoons dry white wine |
| 2 | tablespoons rice vinegar |
| 2 | tablespoons fresh basil, chopped |
| | salt |
| | black pepper, freshly-cracked |

1. In a large saucepan of lightly-salted water, boil edamame until tender, about 4 minutes. Drain well.

2. Heat oil in a large skillet over medium heat. Add pepper, onion, and garlic. Cook, stirring frequently, until vegetables begin to soften, about 2 minutes. Stir in corn, wine, and the edamame. Cook, stirring frequently, until corn is "al dente," about 3 minutes.

3. Remove from the heat. Stir in vinegar and basil. Season with salt and pepper to taste. Transfer the contents of the skillet to a warmed serving bowl, and serve family-style at the center of the table.

# Brussels Sprouts KIMCHI Salad

*makes 8–10 servings*

It's Korea's national dish, and so central to the nation's culture and cuisine that Koreans say "kimchi" instead of "cheese" when posing for photographs. There are many varieties of the dish, each made with a main vegetable ingredient, and at DeepWood Restaurant, Chef Brian Pawlak one-ups the classic form to showcase locally-grown brussels sprouts from Rhoads Farm, brashly garlicky, boldly sour, and accented by the smoky heat of Korean chili powder. "Enjoy this preparation as part of a composed salad," says the chef, "or as an accompaniment to main courses."

## SIDE DISH

| | |
|---|---|
| 4 | cups roughly-chopped brussels sprouts |
| 1 | cup salt |
| | water, as needed |
| 1 | whole daikon radish, thinly-shaved |
| 10 | cloves garlic, minced |
| 4 | tablespoons grated ginger root |
| 3 | ounces fish sauce |
| 1 | bunch chives, minced |
| 1 | bunch green onions, slices |
| 2 | apples, peeled and sliced |
| 4 | tablespoons Korean chili powder |
| 2 | tablespoons sugar |

1. In a large bowl, toss together brussels sprouts and salt. Cover with water and soak, 3 to 6 hours.

2. In a separate bowl, mix together remaining ingredients. Drain and slightly rinse the sprouts. Combine all ingredients and let sit at room temperature for 12 hours or overnight. Refrigerate until ready to serve.

3. To serve, transfer to a chilled bowl and pass family-style around the table.

**According to Mark Twain,** "farming is simply gambling with dirt." But according to Todd Schriver, it's about "living a more balanced and harmonious life."

# ROCK DOVE farm

After growing up on a dairy farm in Indiana, the idealistic young man became a cheesemaker's apprentice on a sheep dairy in Vermont. Still searching for the right fit, Todd tended vegetable gardens on Wayward Seed Farm in Marysville, discovering, in his words, "a new fascination with growing things." In the spring of 2010, a 19th century farmhouse and twenty-three acres in West Jefferson became home to Todd, his wife Heather, and two friendly farm dogs, Louie and Brewster.

Rock Dove Farm is a work in progress. "I'm hoping to get the venture to a size that will allow me to make a decent living," says Todd, "but at the same time not be a slave to it." While the focus is on crop diversity, he is particularly drawn to Italian heirloom varieties.

His mesclun mixes include Lolla Rossa, a curly, light-green Italian lettuce with stunning bright red edges. With seeds from Chioggia, a region in Northern Italy famed for its vegetable production, he grows Radicchio di Chioggia, maroon in color with tight heads and firm leaves, Marina di Chioggia, a beautiful winter squash with rich, sweet, deep yellow-orange flesh, and Chioggia Beets with light red skin and beautiful rings inside, like red and white candy stripes.

Todd has also begun raising rabbits, inspired by a unique heritage breed called Silver Fox, developed during the 1920s in North Canton, Ohio. While they grow into maturity, he puts them to work on the pasture. They eat leftover veggies that don't make it to the Market and turn those scraps into nutrient-rich fertilizer.

"I have many different interests," says Todd, "and if I can work out how to do a lot of small things, that's better than doing one big thing."

"When picking radicchio, look for larger heads with looser outer leaves," says Chef Matt Prokopchak of Trattoria Roma. "Tight, small heads may have been excessively handled and have drier cores. The filling can be changed to your desire – fruit, other vegetables, or nuts (be sure to chop or crush nuts for the mix), and quinoa makes an interesting substitute for the rice."

# Radicchio a la Trattoria

*makes 3 dozen stuffed leaves*

## SIDE DISH

| | |
|---|---|
| 3 | heads radicchio |
| 2 | quarts water |
| 1/2 | cup honey |
| 1/4 | cup salt |
| 4 | ounces finely-chopped onions |
| 3 | garlic cloves, finely-chopped |
| 1 | medium carrot, finely-chopped |
| 3 | ounces arugula, coarsely chopped |
| | olive oil, as needed |
| | butter, as needed |
| 1/4 | teaspoon ground coriander |
| 1/4 | teaspoon ground cumin |
| 1 | teaspoon salt |
| 1 | teaspoon black pepper, freshly-cracked |
| 6 | ounces Marsala wine |
| 1 | pound cooked rice |
| 6 | ounces asiago cheese, grated |

1. Carefully peel outer layers of each radicchio. Cut off bottom of core as need to peel more. Keep peeling until the leaves get smaller and denser. Slice the remainder of the head in half, remove core, and chop the leftover leaves.

2. In a deep pot, bring water to boil with the honey and salt. Lower heat to a simmer, and blanch leaves for 10 to 30 seconds, depending on the texture of the leaves. Remove with a slotted spoon, and let cool on parchment. Do not rinse.

3. For filling, sauté the chopped radicchio with onion, garlic, carrots, and arugula with some olive oil and butter until the vegetables are tender. Season with coriander, cumin, and salt and pepper to taste and deglaze with the wine. Continue to cook until the wine is all but gone.

4. Remove from heat and add cooked rice. Add cheese once mixture is cooled down. (Adding the cooked rice cold will help the mixture cool down faster).

5. To stuff leaves, lay outside of leaf down, so that if there still is any curl left, it faces up. Using your hands, form mix into a football shape and place in leaf. Fold leave over the top, then tuck in outside of leaf, then roll. The leaf should be slightly sticky from honey.

In our view, this is one of the most appetizing and gratifying winter soups ever created. Credit goes to Hubert Seifert, Spagio's chef extraordinaire, for a cozy, warming soup made with Rock Dove Farm's Chiogga beets, Yukon Gold potatoes, tender short ribs of beef – and gracefully capped with crème fraiche and fresh dill. You can make the complete soup a few days ahead; it gets better overnight. Don't add the toppings until just before serving.

# Unforgettable Beet Borscht

*makes 4-6 servings*

## THE BORSCHT

| | |
|---|---|
| 2 | tablespoons canola or vegetable oil |
| 1 | large carrot, peeled and coarsely-chopped |
| 1 | leek (white portion only) sliced in half, rinsed and coarsely-chopped |
| 2 | celery ribs, coarsely-chopped |
| 3 | large beets (approx. 1.5 to 2 lbs), peeled and coarsely-chopped |
| | beef consommé (from left) |
| 2 | medium Yukon Gold potatoes, peeled and diced |
| | shredded beef (from left) |
| | kosher salt |
| | black pepper, freshly-cracked |
| 4–8 | tablespoons crème fraiche, for garnish |
| 2 | tablespoons chopped fresh dill, for garnish |

## THE CONSOMMÉ

| | |
|---|---|
| 3 | pounds beef short ribs, bone-in |
| | mirepoix (diced carrots, leeks, celery) |
| 1 | bay leaf |
| 1 | tablespoon whole peppercorns |

1. In a large stock pot add beef short ribs, mirepoix, bay leaf, and peppercorns. Cover ingredients with enough water to cover by 3". Bring to a boil, then simmer on low for 3 to 4 hours until short ribs are "fork tender."

2. Strain ingredients, reserving beef stock. Remove beef from bones, shred and reserve.

1. Heat oil in a large stock pot. Sauté vegetables (carrot, leek, celery and beets) 3 to 4 minutes on medium-high heat. Stir in reserved consommé & bring to a boil. Reduce heat and lightly simmer until vegetables are "fork tender."

2. Add potatoes and simmer until tender, followed by shredded beef. Simmer until beef is re-heated. Season with salt and pepper to taste.

3. To serve, ladle borscht into 4 to 6 warmed bowls, finishing each with a generous dollop of crème fraîche and a sprinkle of dill.

## The relationship between cook and farmer
is an age-old attraction based on natural synergy –
each needs and wants what the other possesses.
To know the person who produces what you eat is
an invaluable connection.

After her years as a teacher and his years as a furniture builder, Margaret Wince and Rick Myers became culinary herb growers in 1998, inspired, according to Margaret, by the back-to-the-land message promoted in *Mother Earth News*. "Fresh herbs are high value crops," she explains. "There is a potential for small scale farmers to earn a living from limited acreage."

They began wholesaling basil to produce dealers who supplied local restaurants, and by 2000 they were selling a range of herbs at the North Market. When seedlings have become full-grown plants, their small, recyclable pots are inserted into protective plastic sleeves and brought to the Market as "living" herb plants for home gardens. Offerings include "fine herbs," such as basil, chervil, rosemary and thyme, and "robust herbs" like mint, savory, dill and sage.

In addition, Margaret and Rick snip from their own basil patch to sell in bunches at the Market. It's usually harvested early in the morning of market day, making it more appealing to the serious cook. Whether you plant them or pick them up at the Market, adding fresh herbs is a quick way to transform ordinary meals into extraordinary meals.

Basil and garlic are considered the holy grail of pairings, so it's no surprise that Somerset Greenhouse also grows garlic – a hardneck variety called "Killarney Red," whose exceptionally large cloves and the loose skins make it easy to peel. "It has a wonderfully deep, full-bodied flavor," says Margaret. "If this garlic has a cult following, we are steadfast devotees."

somerset
GREEN HOUSE

Mixologist Keith Thompson of Surly Girl Saloon takes his cue from the kitchen and sources herbs from the Market for his culinary cocktail. He combines the scent of juniper berries in local gin with the herbaceous notes of rosemary in a simple syrup, then melds those aromatics with fresh lemon and the effervescence of Champagne. A sophisticated libation for summer entertaining.

# Rosemary's BABY

*makes 1 drink*

## COCKTAIL

| | |
|---|---|
| 1/2 | ounce rosemary simple syrup * |
| 1 | teaspoon lemon juice, freshly-squeezed |
| 1 | ounce Watershed Four Peel Gin |
| | chilled Champagne or other sparkling wine, to top up |
| 1 | rosemary sprig, for garnish |

In a tall flute add rosemary simple syrup, lemon juice, and gin. Top up with Champagne. Garnish with a sprig of rosemary and serve.

*Put ½ cup of sugar and ¼ cup of ground rosemary (use an herb grinder or coffee grinder) into a saucepan with ½ cup of water and bring to a boil. Reduce heat to a simmer, and stir until the sugar dissolves. Take off heat and steep the mixture for 45 minutes. Strain through a fine mesh strainer into a very clean jar and refrigerate until ready to use.

Highly valued for their rich, complex flavor, Somerset's Killarney Red bulbs have 8 or 9 large, easy-to-peel cloves, making them a favorite in the kitchen. It's been said that happiness begins, geographically, where garlic is used in cooking, so this locally-grown hardneck variety – one that becomes almost ambrosial after roasting – helps to make Columbus a more joyful place. Long cooking sweetens pungent garlic. Squeezed out of each clove, the soft garlic is favored with potatoes or spread over rustic bread. To store, place the cloves in an airtight container and pour in enough olive oil to cover the cloves completely. Keep the oil-packed cloves in the refrigerator for up to one week.

# Oven-Roasted
# HARDNECK GARLIC

### GARLIC

| | |
|---|---|
| 1 | head Killarney Red or other hardneck garlic |
| 2 | tablespoons olive oil |

**1.** Preheat the oven to 400° F. Peel away the outer layers of the garlic bulb skin, leaving the skins of the individual cloves intact. Using a small knife, cut ¼" off the top to expose cloves. Place in small baking dish. Add oil and toss to coat.

**2.** Cover tightly with aluminum foil. Bake until garlic skins are golden brown and cloves are tender, about 30 to 40 minutes, or until the cloves feel soft when pressed.

**3.** Allow the heads to cool slightly before handling. Squeeze the soft garlic from the cloves onto your favorite bread and discard the skins.

# Feta Cheese Scones
## with Sun-Dried Tomato and Basil

*makes 6–8 scones*

Follow instructions from Vicki Hink of The Angry Baker for these savory scones with Ohio cheese, sun-dried tomatoes, and fresh basil from Somerset Greenhouse. Crisp and crunchy on the outside, fluffy and moist on the inside, the scones are flecked with fresh green basil throughout, and the tomatoes provide a sweet, chewy tang. Making them even more delectable, feta cheese adds a pleasantly tangy, salty note. Perfect for breakfast, as an addition to the lunchbox or a picnic basket.

### SCONES

| | |
|---|---|
| 2 | cups all-purpose flour |
| 1 | teaspoon salt |
| 1 | tablespoon baking powder |
| 1 | teaspoon black pepper, freshly-cracked |
| 4 | tablespoons cold butter |
| 1 | cup crumbled Lake Erie Creamery Feta cheese |
| 1 | cup sundried tomatoes, chopped |
| 1/2 | cup fresh basil, chopped |
| 3/4 | cup heavy cream, or enough to make cohesive |
| 2 | egg yolks |
| 2 | tablespoons heavy cream |
| 2 | tablespoons parmesan cheese |

1. Preheat oven to 350° F. Lightly grease baking sheet or line with parchment. Whisk together the flour, salt, baking powder, and pepper. Work the butter into the flour until the mixture is crumbly. Mix in the feta, sundried tomatoes, and basil until evenly distributed.

2. Add the cream, stirring to combine. If mixture is too crumbly to stick together, add more cream a tablespoon at a time until it forms a dough ball. Do not over work the dough. Pat the dough into a smooth disk about an inch thick, cut into 6 even wedges and place on prepared baking sheet.

3. Mix two egg yolks with the 2 tablespoons of heavy cream. Brush the mixture on top of scones and sprinkle all scones evenly with parmesan. Bake the scones for 20 to 22 minutes until they are puffed and golden browned on top. Remove from the oven.

4. Bring to the table in a napkin-lined basket or bowl.

STE

**Blueberries have deep roots** in Ohio's agricultural history, some that go back centuries to the Native American tribes. They used the precious berries in many ways – as food, as medicine, even as a dye for clothing.

Inheritor of a family farming tradition, Martin Stehli has set out to master the art of growing blueberries on a favored site in Loudonville, just a few miles from the Mohican Valley. The five-acre patch provides well-drained soil, rich in organic matter deposited by ancient glaciers, and according to Martin, the slope of his "blueberry hill" efficiently drains cold air during frosts. "These are all characteristics that make for a good blueberry farm," he says. "I really kind of lucked out with the location."

Blueberry growers must be willing to practice patience, since the plants don't begin producing fruit until the third season, nor do they become fully productive for another six years. Martin transported his first sizable crop to the Market during the 2012 season, displaying the indigo-colored berries like a proud parent.

A slate-blue, high-bush variety called "Bluecrop" is the backbone of the enterprise – plump, sweet fruit sold by the pint. Bursting with the taste of summer, early-season, light blue "Dukes" are first arrivals, usually by the first week of July, followed by "Spartans," the largest berries of all varieties. Late-ripening, slightly tart "Elliots" extend his offerings at the Market into late September. All three varieties trace their origins to the wild, northern-climate blueberries of Ohio.

Ask him about his passion for growing and selling fresh, local blueberries and he'll tell you, "I love the independence and freedom that comes with making my living on the farm and knowing the value of a hard day's work."

LHI

FARM

"This whole-grain, lightly-sweet treat satisfies breakfast cravings while nourishing your body with wholesome, farm-fresh blueberries," says local veganista Jennie Scheinbach of Pattycake Bakery. "It's gluten-free, no-sugar-added, and, of course, vegan." For a sweeter muffin, top with a light sprinkling of coconut-palm sugar, turbinado or other coarse sugar before baking.

# PATTYCAKE BAKER'S
# Blueberry Muffins

*makes 12 muffins*

## THE MUFFINS

| | |
|---|---|
| 2 | tablespoons ground flax seeds |
| 1/4 | cup water |
| 1/2 | cup unsweetened soymilk |
| 1/2 | cup white grape or apple juice |
| 1 | teaspoon apple cider vinegar |
| 1/2 | cup finely-ground almond meal |
| 1/2 | cup sorghum flour |
| 1/2 | cup millet flour |
| 2 | tablespoons coconut flour |
| 2 | teaspoons baking powder |
| 1/2 | teaspoon baking soda |
| 1/4 | teaspoon sea salt |
| 1/4 | teaspoon guar or xanthan gum (optional; reduce water by tablespoons) |
| 1/4 | cup apple sauce or other fruit pulp (sweet juicer leftovers) |
| 1/4 | cup safflower or other light tasting oil |
| 1 | teaspoon vanilla |
| 8–10 | drops liquid stevia |
| 1 | heaping cup fresh blueberries |

1. In a small bowl, combine ground flax seeds with water and set aside. In a large bowl, mix soymilk, fruit juice, and cider vinegar to curdle.

2. In a medium bowl, measure almond meal, sorghum flour, millet flour, coconut flour, baking powder, baking soda, sea salt, and guar gum, and whisk to fully incorporate.

3. Measure the apple sauce, safflower oil, vanilla, and liquid stevia into the large bowl with the curdled soymilk mixture, including the now thickened flax and water, and whisk to combine.

4. Add the flour mixture to the large bowl of wet ingredients, stirring to fully incorporate. Whisk briskly for 30 seconds. Fold in blueberries and scoop into a lined muffin tin.

5. Bake in preheated 375° F. oven for 22 to 26 minutes or until they are golden and the top bounces back when touched. Cool for about 10 minutes in the tin before turning the muffins out.

## COCKTAIL

| | |
|---|---|
| 8-10 | fresh blueberries |
| | sprig of fresh mint |
| 1 1/2 | ounces **OYO** Vodka |
| 1/2 | ounce Lillet Blanc |
| 1/2 | ounce lime juice, freshly-squeezed |
| 1/2 | ounce simple syrup |
| 3-4 | drops of mint bitters (optional) |

# Staycation

*makes 1 drink*

Muddle mint sprig and blueberries in mixing glass. Build remaining ingredients in the mixing glass with ice. Shake vigorously and pour into rocks glass. Top off with fresh ice.

Waiter, there's a blueberry in my drink! A crisp and refreshing summer cocktail from the blend of OYO, flavorful, plump, fresh blueberries, fresh mint, and a white French aperitif. "I love the brilliant berry color created by muddling the blueberries," says Cris Dehlavi of Middle West Spirits. "The sweet fruit plus the fresh mint make the perfect drink for a midsummer night's cocktail party."

**An avid gardener** at his home in Monticello, Thomas Jefferson wrote, "No occupation is so delightful to me as the culture of the earth, and no culture comparable to that of the garden."

# summer thyme

# FARM

A common passion for growing led Lynn Miller and Delayne Williams to studies at the OSU Agricultural Technical Institute and degrees in horticulture. "We became very good friends," says Delayne, "and we agreed that partnering in a greenhouse business was a good idea." In 2000, the green-thumbed duo set out to grow and cultivate culinary herbs at Summer Thyme Farm in Marysville, and by the following year they were offering an astonishing assortment of plants at the North Market.

Selections include specialty annuals, succulents, veggies, and hanging baskets, but the enterprise is best known for supplying potted culinary herbs for local home gardens – nearly fifty different varieties, carefully labeled and displayed in 3 ½" pots. "While we're not technically organic," explains Lynn, "we do use a natural soy based fertilizer, good environmental practices and crop scheduling to produce healthy, pesticide-free plants."

As early as the tenth century, cooks grew culinary herb gardens for their savory bounty and salad greens. Using herbs in cooking has become one way to enhance healthy, fresh foods and make everyday foods taste great without adding a lot of extra salt or fat.

"There is nothing quite so satisfying as growing your own herbs and using them for the home and family," says Delayne. "For the suburban or inner city apartment with limited room, a well-considered collection of potted herbs can help to create a compact little garden. Even a few pots on the window sill will provide fresh herbs on demand."

"Selling at the Market is the icing on the cake," she admits. "Folks have come to depend on the quality of our plants and our gardening advice. To me, it's especially exciting to get a first-timer started with four of five herbs."

Its glossy, dark-green leaves with distinctively warm, spicy flavors make Genovese basil the best variety for pesto. The word "pesto" itself is a derivation of the Italian word for "pounded," so for the sake of authenticity, it should be made with a mortar and pestle. In this classic version, the leaves are blanched in boiling water, then quickly shocked in ice water, to give the sauce a bright green color and to reduce any bitterness. Spoon over minestrone. Toss with fingerlings for a quick potato salad. Or, of course, serve with pasta – the earthy taste of whole-wheat pasta is *magnifico* with herbaceous pesto.

# "Mortar and Pestle" Pesto Genovese

*makes 1 ½ cups*

## PESTO

| | |
|---|---|
| 3 | cloves garlic, peeled |
| 3/4 | teaspoon sea salt |
| 4 | cups packed basil, blanched briefly in boiling water and shocked in ice water |
| 1/2 | cup extra virgin olive oil |
| 1/2 | cup finely-grated parmesan |
| 1/4 | cup pine nuts, toasted |

1. Pound the garlic and salt together in a mortar and pestle into a smooth paste. Coarsely chop the basil leaves, then add, a handful at a time, and keep grinding using a circular motion until each batch of the leaves is incorporated.

2. Once well-mashed, pound in the olive oil, adding it a spoonful at a time, until well-incorporated.

3. Lastly, pound in the cheese, then the pine nuts. Continue mashing everything for a few minutes until the pesto is as smooth as possible.

# "Live" Mint Julep

*makes 1 drink*

By far the most delicious culinary herb, mint gets all the glory in a time-honored drink that originated in the American South. Lynn and Delayne grow a sweet, aromatic variety of spearmint, actually called "Mint Julep," treasured for the oil in its leaves and best when fresh-picked. The drink is at its peak of flavor the instant it is completed, so there should be just enough liquid in the glass for one or two good swallows. Enthusiasts debate about whether the mint leaves should be muddled or merely steeped in the simple syrup. Either way, a local bourbon adds weight and rich corn, rye and oak notes to the drink. (For crushed ice, wrap ice cubes in a thick towel or cloth bag and hammer away until you have small chunks).

## COCKTAIL

| | |
|---|---|
| 4 | mint leaves + small sprig for garnish |
| 1 | teaspoon powdered sugar |
| 1 1/2 | ounces Watershed Bourbon |
| | crushed ice |
| | splash simple syrup * |

**1.** In the bottom of a julep cup, moisten the mint sprigs and the sugar with a small portion of the bourbon. With the handle of a wooden spoon, gently muddle the leaves to extract the flavor. Fill the glass with crushed ice. Pour in the remaining bourbon. Top with a splash of simple syrup.

**2.** With a long-handled spoon, jiggle (not stir) to chill and mix. Garnish with a sprig of mint.

*Combine 1 cup sugar and 1 cup water in a small saucepan and bring to a boil over medium-high heat, stirring until sugar is dissolved, about 2 minutes. Remove from the heat and cool completely.

**It is said that the small family farm** is one of the last places where men and women can answer the call to be artists, to learn to give love to the work of their hands.

# sunny MEADOWS

After a yearlong apprenticeship at Anderson Orchard in Pickerington, Steve Adams decided that living off of the land didn't seem so far-fetched. Beginning in 2006, he and his wife Gretel set out to till their ten-acre "patch of country in the city," digging a well, burying flower seeds, and building greenhouses to keep the plants growing through the winter.

They use cover crops, plant rotations, homemade compost, beneficial insects, and patient observation to avoid pesticides and chemical fertilizers. "We are a small scale farm with interests in ecology and sustainability rather than organic certification," says Gretel. She and Steve are part of the new local crop of young people redefining what it means to be farmers and reshaping something as old as agriculture.

Sunny Meadows echoes the ethos of the North Market community with flowers that come from local fields and express the cycle of the seasons. In fact, Sunny Meadows Flower Farm is a mere six miles from the Market, and the short field-to-vase journey means that flowers are not only fresher, they are healthier for the people who grow them and healthier for the people who buy and enjoy them.

While they may be accidental farmers, Steve and Gretel have met with success with over one hundred varieties of seasonal, local, sustainable flowers – a rainbow of lilies, lisianthus, dahlias, sunflowers, zinnias, and many more. Transcendentalist Ralph Waldo Emerson suggested that "the earth laughs in flowers," so you might say they bring the joy and beauty of nature to the Market.

# FLO

"Blossoming flowers fresh from the fields invite the warm and welcoming beauty of Spring into the home," says Gretel. "If you are adding tulips to the vase, know that they will grow about an inch as they stretch towards the light. So when arranging, cut them a little shorter than you may have originally planned and watch as the arrangement changes through the week. Everything will open up, showing off the essence of a seasonal flower garden."

## Recipe for a Spring
# FLOWER ARRANGEMENT

### ARRANGEMENT

| | |
|---|---|
| 3 | Asiatic lilies |
| 5 | dusty millers |
| 5 | tulips |
| 5 | anemones |
| 7 | buttercups |
| 7 | reeds rye grass |

In a vase of your choosing, position the largest focal flowers in the heart of the arrangement and slightly lower to give weight, balance, and stability.

Add other flowers to the mix, cutting them to different heights to add interest to the arrangement and make it look more natural than a tight ball of flowers sitting on top of a vase.

Fill in and around the flowers with some foliage. (Herbs work great for filling in, or any other garden items, i.e. hostas, grasses, vines). Work in odd numbers so the arrangement does not appear symmetrical.

Place the arrangement anywhere in your home or office that you choose. Be sure to check the water level at least every couple days and refill as necessary.

VER farm

**It was on a patch of rich upland soil,** six miles south of Zanesville and just west of the Muskingum River, where Dalton Swingle first planted an apple orchard in the 1930s. As a neighbor boy, Bill Thomas helped Mr. Swingle bale hay in the summer and pick apples in the fall. "The first time I ever drove a tractor I was sitting on his lap," recalls Bill. "I was just five years old."

After getting married and graduating from Ohio University, Bill embarked on a teaching career, and when the Swingle orchard came up for sale in 1974, he and wife Vicky settled down on the old place and became apple growers. "My dad always said that money didn't grow on trees," recalls Bill, "but I set out to prove him wrong." Today, they manage over 400 individual trees producing a staggering thirty different apple varieties, but according to Bill, "We don't put all our apples in one basket – we bring peaches, seedless table grapes, plums and blueberries to the North Market as well."

The Market becomes a showcase for the Thomas Family's local, farm-grown fruit. Heirloom apples include sweet, rich Northern Spy and crisp, tangy Grime's Golden. Better sellers are Fugi and Gala, along with Honey Crisp and SunCrisp. Bill is particularly proud of his big, firm Melrose apples with juicy, creamy flesh, a variety developed in the 1940s by the Ohio State Agricultural Experiment Station in Wooster.

Fresh apple cider is one of autumn's great glories, from the first bracing batches, arriving for sale by the second or third week of September. That's when he'll have at least half a dozen varieties, in Bill's words, "enough apples for a good mix." Each week the cider maker selects apples for that week's batch, crafting a balance of sweet, tart, aromatic flavors. Each batch truly reflects the characteristics of the season and fruit.

# THOMAS FAMILY ORCHARD

# "Heaven and Earth"

*makes 4 servings*

In German it's called *Himmel und Erde* which means "Heaven and Earth." You reach up to heaven to pick apples, while turnips and potatoes are pulled from the earth. All three ingredients appear at the Market around the same time, so the dish is truly an expression of the season. Sprinkle with cinnamon and nutmeg for a warm spicy flavor and to honor tradition, serve with sauerkraut and sausage.

## SIDE DISH

| | |
|---|---|
| 3 | medium new potatoes, quartered |
| 2 | small turnips, halved |
| 2 | medium apples, cored, peeled and quartered |
| 1 | tablespoon butter |
| | splash of milk |
| | salt |
| | black pepper, freshly-cracked |

Boil the potatoes and turnips in water until about ¾ done. Add the apples and boil until all ingredients are soft. Drain. With a hand masher or blender, blend with milk and butter until smooth, and season with salt and pepper to taste. Transfer to a warm serving dish and serve family-style around the table.

# Rumor and Innuendo

*makes 1 drink*

Nothing warms cold toes and fingers faster than bourbon, and local cider makes its appearance at the Market just as the weather begins to turn cold. Of course, while stirring bourbon and cider together on their own would be a perfectly tasty beverage, Logan Denny of Mouton adds the heat of jalapeño and a splash of lemon juice to the mix for something truly special.

## COCKTAIL

| | |
|---|---|
| 2 | thin slices of jalapeño pepper |
| 1/4 | ounce freshly-squeezed lemon juice |
| 1 1/2 | ounces bourbon |
| 1 1/2 | ounces local apple cider |
| 1 | teaspoon each of ground cumin and sugar, mixed for garnish |
| | apple slice, for garnish |

1. Muddle jalapeño and lemon juice in the bottom of a cocktail shaker. Add the bourbon and cider and shake vigorously with ice for 10 to 15 seconds.

2. Rim a pre-chilled cocktail glass by moistening the edge with a lemon wedge, then dipping the glass into a small plate of cumin-sugar mix.

3. Double-strain the drink into the sugar-rimmed glass. Garnish with the apple slice and serve.

# "MELROSE" Apple Tart

*makes 1, nine-inch tart*

Apple picking is a cherished rite of fall, a wholesome and fun family outing, and a throw-back to a simpler time when people weren't so disconnected from the production of their sustenance. "Eat them out of hand," says Bill Thomas, "but Melrose apples also make the best dumplings, the best pies, the best crisps." Inspired by the local bounty, Chef Doris Saha of Mozart's Bakery & Piano Café creates a Bavarian-style tart with the "big kahuna" of Thomas Family apples.

## THE CRUST

| | |
|---|---|
| 1/3 | cup butter, softened |
| 1/3 | cup sugar |
| 1/2 | teaspoon vanilla extract |
| 1 | cup all-purpose flour |

Preheat oven to 350° F. Cream butter and sugar until light and fluffy. Mix in vanilla extract and flour until well blended. Press into a 9" tart or spring form pan. Bake for 10 minutes, then remove from oven.

## THE FILLING

| | |
|---|---|
| 8 | ounces cream cheese, softened (1 package) |
| 1/2 | cup sugar |
| 2 | eggs |
| 2 | teaspoons vanilla extract |

Beat cream cheese and sugar until light and fluffy. Add eggs and vanilla until just combined. Spread evenly over prepared crust.

## THE TART

| | |
|---|---|
| 4 | medium Melrose (or other tart) apples, peeled and thinly sliced |
| 1/2 | cup sugar |
| 1 | teaspoon cinnamon |
| 1/2 | teaspoon nutmeg |
| 1/4 | teaspoon cardamom |

Toss apple slices with sugar and spices. Arrange apple slices over filling, making a neat and even pattern. Bake for 40 minutes, until apples are tender. Allow to cool and serve warm or at room temperature.

# Cardamom Bread Pudding
## with "GALA" Apple Compote

*makes 4–6 servings*

"Cardamom is a fragrant spice that pairs well with apples," explains Chef Connor O'Neill of Mezzo, who proves his point with a dish that had its humble beginnings in 13th century England. It was first known as a "poor man's pudding," made from stale leftover bread that was simply moistened in water, to which sugar, spices and other ingredients were added. Notice a pear-like quality in the local, fresh-picked Gala apples, perfect specimens for this delicious dessert.

### THE COMPOTE

| | |
|---|---|
| 1 | stick butter |
| 1/4 | cup brown sugar |
| | pinch cardamom |
| 1 | teaspoon vanilla extract |
| | pinch salt |
| 2 | Gala (or other sweet) apples, peeled and finely-diced |

Heat sauté pan and add butter, sugar, cinnamon, cardamom, vanilla, and salt, and cook 12 minutes. Add apples, and reduce heat to low. Cook, stirring constantly, until creamy. Let cool completely.

### THE PUDDING

| | |
|---|---|
| 1 | quart half-and-half |
| 4 | large eggs |
| 1 | cup brown sugar |
| 1 | teaspoon vanilla extract |
| 1/4 | teaspoon salt |
| 1 | pound chopped bread |
| 1 | teaspoon cardamom ground |
| 1 | pinch ground cinnamon, or to taste |
| | apple compote (from left) |
| | Jeni's Ugandan Vanilla Bean ice cream |

1. Preheat oven to 300° F. Blend half-and-half, eggs, sugar, vanilla extract, and salt in a blender until smooth. Arrange bread in a 9" x 13" baking dish. Add cardamom, cinnamon. Pour egg mixture over bread.

2. Place baking dish in a large roasting pan; fill roasting pan with boiling water halfway up the sides of the baking dish.

3. Place apple compote atop and cover. Bake in preheated oven until set, about 1 ½ hours. Serve warm or cold in individual bowls along with a scoop of Jeni's Ugandan Vanilla Bean ice cream.

# TOAD HILL

**Stop by the Toad Hill stand for a lesson in the diversity of things that can thrive in our region. For twenty seasons at the North Market, locals and visitors have flocked to Tim Patrick's pristine produce with an almost religious fervor.**

He took a circuitous route to becoming an inspirational organic grower. Not all college students who major in Mechanical Engineering become farmers, but Tim left the 100-acre family farmstead, earned a degree, and worked for several years as a consultant to an architectural firm. "I got tired of working in an office," says Tim. "After a while it was too confining, and I was drawn back to the independence I had on the farm."

The complex nature of farming requires both specialized skills and general knowledge, and Tim agrees that his background provides him perspectives that other farmers might miss. "Engineering is about problem-solving and trouble shooting," he explains. "You build a skill set that makes you better than you were when you started."

"We grow things you can't find in other places," says Tim. For one thing, he is unafraid to take risks on crops like artichokes, okra, yard-long gita beans, and a tropical sweetener call stevia. More dependable offerings include a range of heritage fingerling potatoes and a multi-colored assortment of cherry tomatoes.

But Toad Hill might be best-known for the diverse assortment of greens, staggered throughout the season to provide a constant supply to the Market. Offered in mesclun mixes, picturesque salad stews include delicate and succulent baby lettuces with different colors, shapes, and textures, from smooth and tender to frilly and slightly crunchy – compositions that please all the senses.

# FARM

# Plato de Tapas

*makes 6–8 servings*

"For casual entertaining, the tapas experience translates easily to the small home kitchen," according to Chef Jacob Hough of Barcelona Restaurant, who assembles a small dinner party spread focused on Market ingredients. Set out small plates for guests to help themselves. It's a no-frills, stand-up affair as they nibble up a storm from an array of savory dishes. For authenticity, serve chilled Spanish sherry or a youthful Rioja to wash it down.

## THE RADISH SALAD

| | |
|---|---|
| I | pound radishes, sliced on mandolin |
| I | jalapeño pepper, seeded and julienned |
| I | shallot, julienned |
| 2 | oranges, juiced |
| 2 | limes, juiced |
| 1/2 | teaspoon salt |
| 1/2 | teaspoon extra virgin olive oil |
| I | teaspoon black pepper, freshly-cracked |
| 2 | tablespoons sugar |
| 1/2 | teaspoon red wine vinegar |

In a chilled bowl, mix ingredients together. Transfer to a chilled serving platter.

## THE BRUSSELS SPROUTS SALAD

| | |
|---|---|
| I | pound brussels sprouts, blanch and quartered |
| 4 | tablespoons chopped parsley |
| 2 | tablespoons chopped red onion |
| I | teaspoon of salt |
| 2 | garlic cloves, minced |
| I | red bell pepper, chopped |
| 5 | Plum tomatoes, seeded and diced |
| 2 | tablespoons red wine vinegar |
| 1/2 | teaspoon Dijon mustard |
| 1/4 | teaspoon black pepper, freshly-cracked |
| 3 | teaspoons capers |

In a chilled bowl, mix ingredients together. Transfer to a chilled serving platter.

## THE POTATO SALAD

| | |
|---|---|
| 5 | pounds redskin potatoes |
| 1/2 | tablespoon minced garlic |
| 1/2 | tablespoon lemon juice |
| 1/2 | tablespoon Tabasco |
| I | tablespoon Dijon mustard |
| I | tablespoon chopped parsley |
| 1/2 | red onion, diced small |
| 2 | ribs celery, washed and diced |
| 1/8 | cup red wine vinegar |
| 3 | cups mayonnaise |
| | salt |
| | black pepper, freshly-cracked |

Boil potatoes in lightly-salted water until tender. Combine remaining ingredients in a chilled mixing bowl. Drain potatoes. Allow to cool slightly. Dice the cooked potatoes and add to the mixing bowl. Combine well without crushing the potatoes. Season with salt and pepper to taste. Transfer to a warmed serving platter.

In another era, French peasants foraged for wild greens and savory herbs in fields along streambeds and on mountainsides. These "spring mixes," believed to "renew the blood" became the inspiration for mesclun – heirloom salad greens blended for tastes, textures, and colors. The mesclun grower is an artist, capturing the essence of each season. A classic Sunday salad dressing brings Toad Hill Farm's mesclun mix to life; bits of feta cheese add a creamy element, and house-made sweet potato chips provide a delightful crunch.

# Unintimidating Baby Lettuces
## with Sunday Salad Dressing, Feta Cheese and Sweet Potato Chips

*makes 6 servings*

### THE SALAD

| | |
|---|---|
| 16 | ounces mesclun greens, washed, dried, torn into bite-size pieces |
| | Sunday salad dressing (from below) |
| 1/2 | cup crumbled Lucky Penny Farms or other feta cheese |

Divide greens among 6 chilled salad plates. Drizzle about 2 tablespoons of the vinaigrette, and crumble feta cheese over each serving. Garnish salads with the sweet potato chips. Pass the extra vinaigrette alongside.

### THE DRESSING

| | |
|---|---|
| 3 | tablespoons fresh lemon juice |
| 1 | teaspoon Dijon mustard |
| 1 | teaspoon red wine vinegar |
| 1 | clove garlic, minced |
| 1/2 | cup extra virgin olive oil |
| | salt |
| | black pepper, freshly-cracked |

In a small bowl, whisk together lemon juice, mustard, vinegar and garlic. Gradually add oil in a slow, steady stream, whisking until the dressing emulsifies. Season with salt and pepper to taste. Set aside.

### SWEET POTATO CHIPS

| | |
|---|---|
| 4 | cups vegetable oil |
| 1 | sweet potato, peeled, sliced very thin |
| | kosher salt |

1. In a large heavy saucepan, add the vegetable oil and heat to 350° F. Add the potato slices in batches. Fry until light golden brown, turning frequently, about 2 to 3 minutes.

2. Transfer the chips with a slotted spoon to several layers of paper towels to drain and sprinkle them with the salt to taste.

# Tempura of TOAD HILL Chinese Long Beans with Sauce Apropos

*makes 4-6 servings*

More than just a chef, Alana Shock is a philosopher of food. She has established relationships with local farmers and become an integral part of the agricultural community. Often called "the Alice Waters of Columbus," her passion for the North Market influences many of the dishes that come from the kitchen of her eponymous restaurant. "The long beans from Toad Hill Farm are cause for jubilation," says Alana, "at their best when young and slender."

## THE DIPPING SAUCE

| | |
|---|---|
| I | cup low-sodium soy sauce |
| 1/4 | cup sugar |
| 2 | tablespoons minced garlic |
| 2 | tablespoons grated ginger |
| 2 | tablespoons buckwheat or other dark honey |
| 1/2 | cup mirin (rice cooking wine) |
| | pinch of cayenne |
| | chopped scallions, for garnish |

Combine ingredients in a medium pot. Simmer until reduced by one-third. Strain and set aside. Garnish with scallions before serving.

## THE DISH

| | |
|---|---|
| | canola oil, for deep frying |
| 2 | pounds Chinese long beans |
| I | cup all-purpose flour |
| I | tablespoon corn starch |
| I 1/2 | cups seltzer water |

1. Preheat deep fryer to 425° F. Rinse, trim and cut long beans into 2" pieces.

2. Whisk together dry ingredients in a medium bowl (large enough to hold 1 ½ gallons). Set aside.

3. At time to fry, combine wet and dry ingredients and gently mix with tongs until combined, but not smooth. Roll the beans in the tempura batter to coat.

4. heck temperature to make sure it is correct and deep fry the coated beans in 4 batches until golden brown, about 1 ½ minutes per batch. Drain on metal rack or paper towels.

5. To serve, pile tempura beans in the center of warmed plates with a small side bowl of dipping sauce on the side of each.

# TOBY RUN

## He talks about growing mushrooms the way cheesemakers talk about cheeses and wine makers talk about wines. "Growing mushrooms involves science and patience," says Jim Rockwell.

Jim grew up on a farm in Knox County before heading off to study engineering at Franklin University. "I've had the farming bug since I was a kid," he explains, so although he has maintained a career as project engineer for pump manufacturer Warren Rupp in Mansfield, Jim began growing a few vegetable crops for the Market. "It was when I noticed that no one else there was selling mushrooms," he says, "I realized I had an opportunity."

This was not about tracking down wild bunches that spring up at the base of trees, rather it was about establishing a mushroom farm, and Jim sought the guidance of an expert. "A fellow named Scott Ward from nearby Loudonville helped us get started," he explains. "Scott had set up mushroom farms around

the world for food producer Archer Daniels Midland." In 2000, Jim fearlessly embarked on a mushroom farming enterprise with shiitakes and oysters as its centerpiece.

All of his mushrooms grow inside of windowless growing rooms filled with cellulose-rich rye straw. Once the medium is inoculated with spawn, he maintains a sophisticated climate-controlled, isolated environment to encourage maximum fruiting.

With curved, dark brown caps, robust shiitakes have a rich, chewy texture and a distinctive woodsy flavor, inspiring rhapsody among chefs. The more delicate oyster mushrooms (so-called because they resemble oysters) come in colors that vary from snow grey to yellow, with a light, fruity fragrance similar to anise. The level of devotion is evident in the careful way in which Jim displays his offerings – arranged together like little mushroom bouquets.

# GROWERS

Ceramic plates continue to emit heat for a long time after removal from their heat sources. In this simple dish, a variety of mushrooms are partially cooked in the kitchen, then brought to the table in the "toban" ceramic plate to finish cooking. The trick is to work quickly so that the mushrooms do not overcook. Serve the dish promptly to fully savor the spectrum of textures, aromas and flavors. At Toby Run, Jim grows mushrooms that are a brilliant proof that Nature is the ultimate chef.

# Mushroom Toban Yaki

*makes 2 servings*

## SIDE DISH

| | |
|---|---|
| 10 | ounces assorted mushrooms |
| | grapeseed oil, as needed |
| 2 | tablespoons clarified butter |
| 2 | tablespoons sake |
| 1 | tablespoon light soy sauce |
| 1 | tablespoon yuzu juice |

**1.** Remove the base part of the shiitake mushroom stems. Cut all the mushrooms into bite-size pieces. Flash-broil to partially cook. Heat a toban (hotplate) thoroughly over a high heat. Pour a bit of grapeseed oil into the toban, add the clarified butter, followed by the mushrooms. Mix in the sake, soy sauce, and the yuzu juice.

**2.** Remove from heat and cover with the toban lid, removing when ready to eat.

French for "good wife," *bonne femme* describes a dish prepared in an uncomplicated, homey manner. In this Market-inspired notion of a French country classic, the refined flavor of sole is emphasized by a generous portion of Toby Run mushrooms, poached with the fish in luscious Chardonnay from Ohio's northernmost growing region. Try the same preparation with flounder, haddock, halibut, or cod. What to drink: For perfect compatibility with the dish, serve remainder of the Chardonnay and uncork a second bottle.

# SOLE "Bonne Femme" with Oyster Mushrooms

*makes 4 servings*

## MAIN DISH

| | |
|---|---|
| 4 | sole fillets, rinsed and dried |
| 1/4 | pound oyster mushrooms, sliced |
| 2 | shallots, minced |
| 2 | teaspoons fresh chives, chopped |
| 1/3 | cup Ferrante "Grand River Valley" Chardonnay or other dry white wine |
| 1 1/2 | tablespoons unsalted butter |
| | salt and pepper, to taste |

1. In a wide sauté pan set over medium heat, melt butter and sauté mushrooms, 4 to 5 minutes. Add shallots and wine, and season with salt and pepper. Add the fish to the pan and bring to a boil. Lower the heat to medium, and simmer for 10 minutes, covered, or until the fish flakes easily with a fork.

2. To serve, arrange the fillets in the center of each of 4 warmed dinner plates and spoon some of the mushrooms and pan juices around each serving.

**Moviegoers will recall** Bellefontaine as the setting for *The Old-Fashioned Way*, in which W.C. Fields plays the "Great McGonigle." This Logan County city is also home to a farming enterprise that has been in the hearts and hands of the same family for four generations.

# WISHWELL FARMS PRODUCE

At the turn of the last century, John Wish began farming with just a few cows and some Dutch pragmatism. The farm was passed down to his sons, with Frank operating a dairy and Paul growing sweet corn. Paul's son, Jim, turned to grain growing, and his son, Jason, diversified the 75-acre farm by cultivating a wide range of vegetables.

Succulent sweet corn is a strategic crop, depending on early, mid-, and late-season varieties to extend the harvest. "Succession plantings are important," says Jason, "but tender, good-tasting corn is the result of breeding, with dozens of new and ever-sweeter cultivars that retain their sugar content for days." First arriving ears of corn at the Market are "Sweet Temptations," a reliable hybrid variety Jason calls his workhorse, and in his words, "It gets us going out the gate."

Tomatoes, both hydroponic greenhouse-grown and field-grown, include "Charger," a brilliant red, very firm, high yielding salad tomato, and "Phoenix," a globe-shaped, large to extra-large, good-tasting fruit. Bursting with umami and sweetness, Wishwell tomatoes have developed an almost cult following at the Market.

"Living in harmony with the land is a way of life that I inherited," says Jason, "and one that I will be proud to pass on to my children." Sustainable farming means that pesticides are used minimally and only when necessary. "I'm not just growing to try to sell everything I can to make a living," he says. "I care about what I eat and how I grow the food that feeds my own family."

The appearance of Wishwell Farms' sweet corn at the Market inspires an *antojito* designed to satisfy a craving – griddle cakes, prepared with masarepa, a pre-cooked corn flour. Shaved sheep milk cheese from the Sippel Family Farm in Mount Gilead adds a salty contrast, and the result is striking. These arepas make a wonderful breakfast served with farm-fresh fried eggs and a side of chorizo.

# Sweet Corn Arepas with "Kokoborrego" Sheep Milk Cheese

*makes 8–10 pancakes*

## SIDE DISH

| | |
|---|---|
| 1 3/4 | cups milk |
| 1 1/2 | cups fresh sweet corn kernels (from about 3 ears of sweet corn) |
| 2 | tablespoons butter + extra for sautéing |
| 2 | cups masarepa |
| 1/2 | cup Kokoborrego "Owl Creek Tomme" or other sheep cheese, shaved salt, to taste |

**1.** Place the milk and the corn kernels in a blender and pulse until coarsely ground. Pour the corn/milk mixture into a saucepan and add 2 tablespoons of butter. Heat over medium heat until milk just comes to a boil. Remove from heat and let cool for 2 minutes.

**2.** Add the masarepa to a large bowl. Whisk in the cheese. With a wooden spoon, gradually pour the hot milk mixture into the masarepa. Stir mixture until cool enough to handle, then knead gently by hand into a smooth, homogenous dough. Season with salt and knead.

**3.** To shape, take a small handful of the dough and form it into a ball. Flatten into a pancake shape, about 1/3" thick and about 4 inches in diameter. Repeat with remaining dough.

**4.** Melt butter in a large skillet over medium-low heat. Cook pancakes in batches until golden brown and crispy on both sides, about 4 minutes per side.

**5.** To serve, transfer to a warmed serving platter and pass family-style around the table.

"Smoked tomatoes have a wonderfully intense aroma and flavor," explains Chef Phil Gulis of Plate, "and I wanted to use them in a dish that would show off their unique character." There is sweetness from the concentrated fruit sugars, natural acidity, and of course, a jolt of smoke, which is what really elevates this tangy marriage of local tomatoes, onions, and peppers. A refreshing, sweet-and-savory salsa accompanies the dish rather nicely.

# Cherry Wood Smoked Tomato Gazpacho with Watermelon Salsa

*makes 4 servings*

### FOR SMOKING ON AN OUTDOOR GRILL

Ignite gas or charcoal to medium heat. Place damp smoking chips as close to the heat source as possible by either wrapping a grill plate with foil or creating a foil "pouch" for the chips. When smoke begins to rise from the chips, place quartered tomatoes, skin side down, on the top grill plates and close the lid. Allow to smoke for at least 20 minutes, longer to achieve more intense flavor.

### FOR STOVE-TOP SMOKING ON A GAS STOVE

Line the bottom of an 8"x 8" aluminum disposable pan with damp cherry wood smoking chips. Place quartered tomatoes, skin side down, on a perforated pan (or second aluminum pan with small holes throughout the bottom) and cover with aluminum foil. Heat the smoking chips over medium heat. When the smoke begins to rise from the chips place your covered tomatoes on top. (Be sure the tomatoes are covered completely to prevent excess smoke from circulating in your kitchen). Lower the heat and allow to smoke for at least 20 minutes, longer to achieve more intense flavor.

## FOR THE SALSA

| | |
|---|---|
| 1 | cup watermelon, finely chopped |
| 2 | tablespoons red onion, minced |
| 2 | tablespoons celery, minced |
| | salt |
| | black pepper, freshly-cracked |
| | sugar, if needed |
| | extra virgin olive oil, as needed |
| 4–5 | large basil leaves, finely chopped |

**1.** Place watermelon, red onion, and celery in a mixing bowl and season with salt and pepper to taste. (If the watermelon you are using is not as naturally sweet as you would like, add a small amount of sugar).

**2.** Just before serving, toss mix with olive oil and basil.

## THE GAZPACHO

| | |
|---|---|
| 4 | large heirloom tomatoes, quartered and smoked (from left) |
| 1/4 | cup red onion, roughly chopped |
| 1/4 | cup bell pepper, roughly chopped for extra heat, use a jalapeño pepper |
| 3 | cups tomato juice |
| 1/4 | cup extra virgin olive oil |
| 2 | tablespoons sherry vinegar |
| | salt |
| | black pepper, freshly-cracked |
| | watermelon salsa (from left) |

**1.** Place smoked tomatoes, red onion, and bell pepper in a blender and puree while slowly adding tomato juice, until smooth. Combine with olive oil, vinegar, and season with salt and pepper to taste. Place in non-metal, non-reactive storage container, cover tightly and refrigerate overnight, allowing flavors to blend.

**2.** To serve, ladle into 4 chilled bowls and spoon desired amount of salsa onto the center of each gazpacho.

# INDEX

## SOUPS

| | |
|---|---|
| I.P.A. "Candy Onion" Soup | 128 |
| Alex's Cheeseburger Soup | 64 |
| Fragrant Fish Soup with Tamarind and Sambal | 77 |
| Spicy Popcorn Soup | 103 |
| Chef Hubert Seifert's Pumpkin Soup | 163 |
| Tortilla Soup with Fried Farm Eggs | 168 |
| Unforgettable Beet Borscht | 182 |
| Cherry Wood Smoked Tomato Gazpacho with Watermelon Salsa | 212 |

## SMALL PLATES

| | |
|---|---|
| Zucchini Pronto | 132 |
| Asparagus "Gremolata" | 119 |
| Brünhilde on a Brezel | 19 |
| Amish Farmstead Potatoes with Onions, Peppers, and Garlic | 129 |
| Bodega "Whiskey Dip" | 31 |
| Fonduta di Piemonte | 32 |
| Buffalo Fried Oysters with Crumbled Bleu Cheese | 38 |
| Ploughman's Lunch | 41 |
| Loaded Potato Chips for "The Cheese Man" with Gorgonzola-Parmesan-Garlic Sauce | 42 |
| Parmesan Crème Brûlée with Caramelized Rosemary-Sugar Crust | 43 |
| "Summer Brunch" Granola with Local Strawberries and Maple Whipped Cream | 142 |
| "Goi Cuon" Summer Rolls with Peanut Dipping Sauce | 78 |
| Granville Inn's Toasted Cheese | 156 |
| Rillettes de Canard | 157 |
| "Yard Bird" Burgers with Avocado Mayonnaise | 90 |
| Chicken Spiedies with "Truck Dust" | 93 |
| "French Breakfast" Radish Tartine on Rustic French Bread | 97 |
| "Strata" Breakfast Casserole | 98 |
| "Black Jewell" Popcorn with Garlic and Herb Butter | 102 |
| "Pumpkin Pie" Pancakes | 164 |
| Heirloom Tomato "Salsa Bandara" | 131 |
| Hummus Quinoa Patty with Pickled Vegetables and Black Bean & Corn Relish | 176 |

| | |
|---|---|
| Radicchio a la Trattoria | 181 |
| Feta Cheese Scones with Sun-Dried Tomato and Basil | 187 |
| Oven-Roasted Hardneck Garlic | 186 |
| Oysters Diavolo | 53 |
| "Heaven and Earth" | 199 |
| Plato de Tapas | 203 |
| Mushroom Toban Yaki | 207 |
| Sweet Corn Arepas with "Kokoborrego" Sheep Milk Cheese | 211 |
| Tempura of Toad Hill Chinese Long Beans with Sauce Apropos | 205 |

## SALADS AND SIDES

| | |
|---|---|
| "Earth Day" Salad with Asparagus and Poached Egg | 120 |
| Chow-Chow for Hot Dogs | 20 |
| Cilantro-Jalapeño "Hot Mess" with Sriracha | 124 |
| Crispy Oven-Roasted Kale | 127 |
| Le Chou Rouge Braisé | 39 |
| "Pickle Barrel" Fried Dills | 65 |
| Not Like Any Other Slaw, Man! | 67 |
| "Fall Harvest" Honey-Roasted Root Vegetables | 145 |
| Crispy Brussels Sprouts with Honey, Lemon, Chili, and Almonds | 148 |
| Wilted Malabar Spinach "Scented with Garlic" | 151 |
| Parsley, Sage, Rosemary and Thyme Salad with Slow-Poached Eggs | 169 |
| "Chintz Room" Chicken Salad with Toasted Pecans | 159 |
| "Brandywine" Panzanella with Local Goat Cheese | 171 |
| Sweet Summer Corn and Edamame "Succotash" | 178 |
| Brussels Sprouts Kimchi Salad | 179 |
| Pizzeria "Rocket" Salad | 111 |
| Salade Liègeoise | 115 |
| Champagne-Braised Jicama Salad | 17 |
| "Local Roots" Composed Salad | 60 |
| Chop Chop Salad with Chimichurri | 113 |
| Unintimidating Baby Lettuces with Sunday Salad Dressing | 204 |

## MAIN DISHES

| | |
|---|---|
| Seared Scallops with Hot Pepper Cream | 123 |
| Momma Seifert's Meatloaf with Bacon-Infused Mashed Potatoes | 27 |
| Grilled Garlic-Rubbed Rack of Lamb with Warm Vegetable Salad | 26 |
| Pork Osso Bucco with Chianti-Roasted Root Vegetables | 28 |
| Grilled Flank Steak with Cucumber Aioli Marinade | 136 |
| Coq au Vin with Saffron | 135 |
| Pasta Carbonara with Davidson Farm Bacon | 138 |
| Tunisian Chicken Stew | 49 |
| Mixed Vegetable Korma | 55 |
| Smoked Pork Chops with Red Wine Gastrique | 68 |
| "Bigos" Polish Hunter's Stew with Horseradish Sour Cream | 72 |
| Grilled "Asian Bride" Eggplants with Sweet Red Peppers | 152 |
| Pad Thai, North Market-Style | 84 |
| Chef Hubert Seifert's Roast Turkey with Bread Pudding | 89 |
| Braised Chicken with Tuscan Aroma | 91 |
| Salmon Grilled on Cedar Shakes with Applewood-Smoked Salt | 94 |
| "Thursday" Potato Gnocchi with Tomato-Rosemary Broth | 106 |
| Deconstructed Ratatouille | 172 |
| Best-Ever Mussels and Frites | 16 |
| Pan-Fried Lake Erie Walleye with Peppered Shallot Cream Sauce | 52 |
| Whole Grain Risotto with Shiitake Mushrooms and Kale | 59 |
| Sole "Bonne Femme" with Oyster Mushrooms | 208 |
| A Warming Winter Risotto | 87 |
| "Mortar and Pestle" Pesto Genovese | 193 |
| Crispy Pig Tails with Market Hot Pepper Sauce | 160 |
| Punjabi Chole | 56 |

## DESSERTS

| | |
|---|---|
| Chocolate-Espresso Madeleines | 16 |
| Amish Apple Butter Doughnuts | 23 |
| "After School" Cookie Plate | 46 |
| Frozen Tessora Soufflé with Local Raspberry Coulis | 143 |
| Honey and Lavender Cupcakes with Honey-Vanilla Buttercream Frosting | 147 |
| Polish "Angel Wings" | 71 |
| Pattycake Baker's Blueberry Muffins | 190 |
| "Melrose" Apple Tart | 200 |
| Cardamom Bread Pudding with "Gala" Apple Compote | 201 |
| The Buckeye State Banana Split | 75 |

## BEVERAGES AND COCKTAILS

| | |
|---|---|
| Caffè con Cioccolato | 11 |
| Poblano Escobar | 125 |
| The Dave | 135 |
| "Old Wives' Tale" Hot Toddy | 35 |
| The Hibiscus Bee's Knees | 146 |
| "Tom Yum" Bloody Mary | 83 |
| Blood Orange "Aperitivo" | 105 |
| "Theobroma" Hot Chocolate with Cayenne Whipped Cream | 109 |
| Noir 75 | 175 |
| Dino's "Flame of Love" | 111 |
| Rosemary's Baby | 185 |
| Staycation | 191 |
| Rumor and Innuendo | 199 |
| "Live" Mint Julep | 194 |
| Mayday | 95 |